taste of Asia

taste of
Asia

a tantalizing taste of the exotic Far East

steven wheeler

HERMES
HOUSE

This edition is published by Hermes House

Hermes House is an imprint of Anness Publishing Ltd
Hermes House, 88–89 Blackfriars Road, London SE1 8HA
tel. 020 7401 2077; fax 020 7633 9499; info@anness.com

© Anness Publishing Limited 1994, 2002

Published in the USA by Hermes House, Anness Publishing Inc.
27 West 20th Street, New York, NY 10011; fax 212 807 6813

A CIP catalogue record for this book is available from the British Library.

Publisher Joanna Lorenz
Project Editor Lindsay Porter
Photographer Edward Allwright
Styling Maria Kelly
Design David Rowley Design
Cover Design Axis Design Editions Ltd

Previously published as *Classic Asian Cooking*

1 3 5 7 9 10 8 6 4 2

NOTES
For all recipes, quantities are given in both metric and imperial measures and,
where appropriate, measures are also given in standard cups and spoons. Follow
one set, but not a mixture, because they are not interchangeable.

Standard spoon and cup measures are level.
1 tsp = 5ml, 1 tbsp = 15ml, 1 cup = 250ml/8fl oz

Australian standard tablespoons are 20ml. Australian readers should use 3 tsp in
place of 1 tbsp for measuring small quantities of gelatine, cornflour, salt, etc.

Medium eggs are used unless otherwise stated.

CONTENTS

INTRODUCTION

Varied as the recipes of South-east Asia are, they all have three things in common: a tradition of perfect ingredients, a commitment to making each dish a celebration in taste, and a keen eye for exquisite presentation. This book provides a valuable insight into the cooking of Thailand, Vietnam, Malaysia, Singapore, Indonesia, the Philippines and Japan, revealing how each country has established its own unique style. With a wide variety of South-east Asian produce now available in Western supermarkets, there is every opportunity to explore and enjoy at home dishes that have long been a culinary way of life in the East as well as a source of delight in the restaurants of the West.

THE PRINCIPLES OF SOUTH-EAST ASIAN COOKING

The cuisines of the countries of South-east Asia vary considerably, from the Spanish-influenced dishes of the Philippines to the dietary demands of the Buddhist and Muslim faiths. One practice common to most countries is the method of serving. Mealtimes are relaxed, informal affairs, with all dishes arriving at the table at the same time. Guests help themselves, either with chopsticks or with the left hand. Dishes should offer a balance of textures and aromas, and ingredients must be fresh and flavoursome.

EQUIPMENT AND UTENSILS

Bamboo skewers (1) Bamboo skewers are widely used for barbecues and grilled (broiled) foods. They are disposed of after use.

Chopping board (2) It is worth investing in a solid chopping board. Thick boards provide the best surface and will last for many years.

Citrus zesting tool (3) The outer peel or zest of citrus fruit imparts a distinctive flavour to many South-east Asian dishes. This tool is designed to remove the zest while leaving behind the bitter white pith of the fruit.

Cleavers (4, 5) At first sight cleavers may look and feel out of place for domestic use, but they are ideally suited to fine chopping and transferring ingredients from chopping board to wok. Small cleavers are used mostly for chopping and shredding fruits and vegetables. They can also be used for the preparation of meat and fish.

Cooking chopsticks (6) Extra long chopsticks can be used to stir ingredients in the wok. Their length permits you to keep at a distance from the cooking ingredients.

Draining wire (7) Draining wires are designed to rest on the side of a wok. They are used mainly for deep-frying.

Food processor (8) The food processor is a useful alternative to the more traditional pestle and mortar, and is suitable for grinding wet spices.

Large chopping knife (9) If you are not comfortable using a cleaver, a large Western-style chopping knife can be used instead. Choose one with a deep blade to give you the best control.

Rice paddle (10) These are generally made from a large section of bamboo. Rice paddles are used to stir and fluff rice after cooking. A pair of chopsticks may also be used for fluffing rice.

Rice saucepan and lid (11) A good rice saucepan with a close-fitting lid is an essential piece of equipment for South-east Asian cooking. Stainless steel pans with a heavy base are best.

Sharpening stone (12) Sharpening stones are used for sharpening knives and cleavers. They are available from hardware stores and should be immersed in water before use.

Stainless steel skimmer (13) Stainless steel skimmers should be used when strong flavours are likely to affect bare metal utensils.

Wire skimmer (14) Wire skimmers are used to retrieve cooked food from boiling water or hot fat. Bare metal skimmers can retain strong flavours and are therefore not recommended for use with fish-based liquids.

Wok (15) The wok is used in all parts of South-east Asia. The shape of the wok allows deep-frying and stir-frying in a minimum of fat, thus retaining the freshness and flavour of ingredients.

Wok ladle (16) Wok ladles are used to stir liquid ingredients while cooking. They are also useful for transferring cooked food to serving bowls.

Wok lid (17) Wok lids have a large domed surface and are designed to retain moisture given off during cooking. The steam held beneath the lid is often used to keep ingredients from taking on too much colour when frying.

Wok scoop (18) The wok scoop is designed to make contact with the curved surface of the wok. Most scoops are made of stainless steel and will not retain strong flavours.

INGREDIENTS

Acorn squash (1) Many varieties of squash and pumpkin are grown in South-east Asia. They are used mainly as a vegetable, but may sometimes be used in desserts.

Aubergine (egg plant) (2) The dark-skinned aubergine (egg plant) is included in a variety of slow-cooking dishes and is renowned for its smooth texture. Large aubergines can be bitter and should be salted before use.

Banana leaves (3) The banana leaf is widely used for wrapping ingredients before cooking. If banana leaves are unavailable use aluminium foil.

Cardamom pods (4) Cardamom is a member of the ginger family. The sweetest flavour is contained in the seed of the olive-green pods and is usually ground with other spices. Large black pods have a bitter flavour and combine well with sweet curry ingredients.

Celophane noodles (bean thread noodles) (5) These fine noodles are usually made from mung bean flour, although some varieties contain rice, soy and pea starch. When boiled, they have a smooth texture and are an important ingredient for spring roll stuffings. Celophane noodles become crispy when deep-fried.

Chillies (6) Used in moderation, chillies provide the hot sweet glow typical of many South-east Asian curries and dipping sauces. As a rule, small chillies are the hottest and green varieties tend to be less sweet than red.

Chinese red onions (shallots) (7) The Chinese red onion has a strong flavour despite its small size. If unavailable, use golden shallots or an increased quantity of white onions.

Cinnamon (cassia) (8) Tightly-curled cinnamon has a smooth, warm flavour which is given to sweet and savoury cooking. Cassia, pictured here, has a more robust flavour and is used with other strong spices.

Coconut (9) The coconut is essential to many dishes of South-east Asia. Coconut milk is obtained from the white flesh of the nut and is both rich and smooth-tasting.

Coriander leaf (10) Fresh coriander has a strong, pungent smell that combines well with other rich flavours. The white coriander root is used when the green colouring is not required. Bunches of coriander will keep for up to five days in a jar of water. Cover with a plastic bag and store in the refrigerator.

Coriander seeds (11) Coriander is common to all styles of cooking throughout South-east Asia. The seeds are dry-fried with other spices to release the unique flavour.

Cumin seeds (12) Cumin has a similar ribbed shape to fennel seed and comes from the parsley family. It has a warm, heady flavour that combines well with coriander and is widely used in beef dishes. Cumin seeds are usually dry-fried before use.

Egg noodles (13) Egg noodles are made from wheat flour and are sold dried in single portions. When cooked, egg noodles are used in dishes such as Mee Goreng from Singapore and Pansit Guisado from the Philippines.

Enokitake mushrooms (14) These slender mushrooms have a sweet, peppery taste and are used to enhance the clear broths of Japan. Enokitake can also be eaten raw as a salad ingredient.

Fennel seeds (15) Plump green fennel seeds are similar in character to cumin, and have a sweet aniseed flavour. The seeds combine well with peanuts and the zest of citrus fruit, and are an aid to digestion.

Fermented shrimp paste (Blachan, Kapi) (16) The smell of fermented shrimp paste by itself is quite repellent, but when blended with other spices, shrimp paste loses its unpleasant flavour and provides the unique taste and character typical of many South-east Asian sauces.

Galingal (17) Galingal is a member of the ginger family and grows in a similar root shape. The fibrous root has a resinous quality similar to pine and combines well with fish dishes. Dried galingal is increasingly available. It should be soaked in boiling water before use.

Garlic (18) Garlic marries well with the strong pungent flavours of the East. Individual cloves can be finely chopped or crushed in a garlic press.

Ginger (19) Fresh ginger is well-known in the West for its warm, pungent flavour. In its native region of South-east Asia, it features in many intriguing spice combinations.

Lime leaves (20) Lime leaves are an essential part of many slow-cooking dishes. The deep, citrus flavour of the leaf combines especially well with rich coconut milk and hot chilli spices.

Limes (21) Limes are widely used to add sharpness to finished dishes. Wedges are often served at the table so that guests may season dishes to taste.

Lemon grass (22) Fresh lemon grass is common to many dishes throughout South-east Asia. Its flavour has a rich lemon quality that combines well with other wet spices. Lemon grass is also available dried.

Lychees (23) The brittle skin of this fine fruit peels away like the shell of a boiled egg. The white scented fruit has a clean fresh taste and is served at the end of a meal.

Mandarin oranges (24) The flavour obtained from the outer zest of the mandarin orange combines well with the rich spices of the East. Satsumas and clementines are also suitable.

Mango (25) The mango offers a rich scented flavour to both sweet and savoury dishes. Mangoes are ripe when the green skin is flushed with red.

Mint (26) Varieties of mint feature in the cooking of Vietnam. The fresh flavour combines particularly well with coriander leaf, peanuts and the zest of mandarin orange. Mint is also used in sweet and savoury fruit salads.

Moolie (27) The giant white radish is common to many Japanese dishes and is ideal for making flower garnishes. If unavailable, white turnip or red radish may be substituted.

Nutmeg (28) The flavour of nutmeg is obtained by grating the nut on a fine grater. The fresh oils that are released provide strength and character to many well-known spice mixtures.

Pickled ginger (29) Thinly-sliced pink pickled ginger is served as a condiment with Japanese sushi, grilled fish and beef. It has a warm, sweet flavour and is found in most oriental food stores.

Pineapple (30) Pineapple offers a clean refreshing flavour and is an aid to digestion. It may be served at the end of a meal, or as an ingredient in a main dish.

Seaweed (31) Dried seaweed is widely used in Japanese cooking to impart a salty, rich flavour of the sea. Nori is a dried, flat seaweed used for making sushi. Kelp is also dried and should be soaked in water before use.

Sesame seeds (32) White sesame seeds are widely used in Japanese cooking. The seeds should be dry-fried, to release their flavour. Toasted seeds are often ground finely to thicken and enrich sauces.

Shiitaki mushrooms (33) Fresh shiitaki mushrooms have a rich, meaty flavour that combines especially well with shellfish and poultry. Shiitake are widely available dried and yield a good flavour when soaked in boiling water.

Sichuan pepper (34) Sichuan pepper has a warm, fruity flavour without the intense heat of white or black peppercorns. To obtain the best flavour, Sichuan pepper should be dry-fried and coarsely ground before use.

Somen noodles (35) Somen noodles are made from wheat flour and are an important part of the Japanese diet. It is most common to find somen noodles in a flavoursome chicken broth.

Spring onions (scallions) (36) Spring onions (scallions) have a milder flavour than onions and are suited to dishes that are cooked quickly. Both the white and green parts are used.

Star anise (37) This attractive spice is sold in star-shaped pods and carries the soft scent of aniseed. The pods are used whole or ground to flavour sweet and savoury dishes.

Star fruit (38) Star fruit have a sweet scented flavour when ripe and can be eaten cooked or raw in fruit salads.

Sweet potato (39) The sweet richness of this red tuber marries well with the hot and sour flavours of South-east Asia. In Japan, the sweet potato is used to make delicious candies and sweetmeats.

Tomatoes (40) Both ripe and under-ripe tomatoes feature in the cooking of South-east Asia. Under-ripe fruit are used in slow-cooking meat dishes and lend a special sour taste.

HOT CHILLI DUCK WITH CRAB MEAT AND CASHEW NUT SAUCE

Bhed Sune Khan

This dish may be served with Thai rice and a dish of Thai Dipping Sauce.

SERVES 4–6 **Ingredients** 2.7kg/6lb duck 1.1 litre/2 pints/5 cups water, to cover 2 lime leaves 1 tsp salt 2–3 small red chillies, seeded and finely chopped	5 tsp sugar ½ tsp salt 2 tbsp coriander seeds 1 tsp caraway seeds 115g/4oz raw cashew nuts, chopped 1 piece lemon grass, 7.5cm/3in long, shredded 1 piece galingal or fresh ginger, 2.5cm/1in long, peeled and finely chopped 2 cloves garlic, crushed	4 shallots, or 1 medium onion, finely chopped 1 piece shrimp paste, 2cm/¾in square 25g/1oz coriander white root or stem, finely chopped 175g/6oz frozen white crab meat, thawed 50g/2oz creamed coconut 1 small bunch coriander, chopped, to garnish

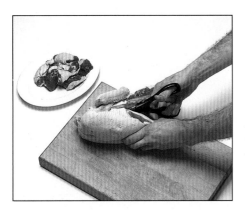

1 To portion the duck into manageable pieces, first remove the legs. Separate the thighs from the drumsticks and chop each thigh and drumstick into 2 pieces. Trim away the lower half of the duck with kitchen scissors. Cut the breast piece in half down the middle, then chop each half into 4 pieces.

2 Put the duck flesh and bones into a large saucepan and cover with the water. Add the lime leaves and salt, bring to the boil and simmer, uncovered, for 35–40 minutes, until the meat is tender. Discard the duck bones, skim off the fat from the stock and set aside.

3 To make the curry sauce, grind the red chillies together with the sugar and salt using a pestle and mortar or a food processor. Dry-fry the coriander and caraway seeds and the cashew nuts in a wok to release their flavour, about 1–2 minutes. Add the chillies, the lemon grass, galingal or ginger, garlic and shallots or onion and reduce to a smooth paste. Add the shrimp paste and coriander.

4 Add a cup of the liquid in which the duck was cooked and blend to make a thin paste.

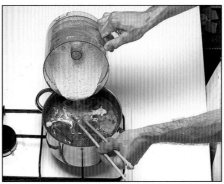

5 Stir the curry seasoning in with the duck, bring to the boil and simmer, uncovered, for 20–25 minutes.

6 Add the crab meat and creamed coconut and simmer briefly. Turn out onto an attractive serving dish, decorate with chopped coriander.

THAI GRILLED CHICKEN

Kai Yang

Thai grilled chicken is especially delicious when cooked on the barbecue. It should be served with a dipping sauce.

SERVES 4–6	4 tsp sugar	3 tbsp vegetable oil
	2 tsp paprika	salt, to season
Ingredients	I piece fresh ginger, 2cm/¾in long	6–8 lettuce leaves, to serve
900g/2lb chicken drumsticks or thighs	3 cloves garlic, crushed	½ cucumber, cut into strips, to garnish
I tsp whole black peppercorns	15g/½oz coriander, white root or stem, finely	4 spring onions (scallions), trimmed, to garnish
½ tsp caraway or cumin seeds	chopped	2 limes, quartered, to garnish

1 Chop through the narrow end of each drumstick with a heavy knife. Score the chicken pieces deeply to allow the marinade to penetrate. Set aside in a shallow bowl.

2 Grind the peppercorns, caraway or cumin seeds and sugar in a pestle and mortar or a food processor. Add the paprika, ginger, garlic, coriander and oil and grind.

3 Spread the marinade over the chicken and chill for 6 hours. Cook the chicken under a moderate grill for 20 minutes, turning once. Season, arrange on lettuce, and garnish.

THAI CHICKEN AND PRAWN (SHRIMP) SOUP

Tom Yum Gung

In Thailand a soup such as this is often served with a dry curry to help balance the texture of the curry dish.

SERVES 4–6	I piece lemon grass, 7.5cm/3in long	2 lime leaves
	2 cloves garlic, crushed	225g/8oz fresh or cooked prawn (shrimp) tails,
Ingredients	2 tbsp chopped coriander root, or stem	peeled and de-veined
2 × 175g/6oz chicken breasts, on the bone	2–3 small red chillies, seeded and finely	juice of I lime
½ chicken stock cube	chopped	4 sprigs coriander, chopped, to garnish
400g/14oz canned coconut milk	2 tbsp fish sauce	2 spring onions (scallions), green part only, sliced,
I piece galingal or fresh ginger, 2cm/¾in long	5 tsp sugar	to garnish
finely chopped	½ tsp salt	4 large red chillies, sliced, to garnish

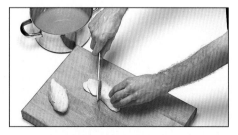

1 Cover the chicken with water, add stock cube, and simmer for 45 minutes. Slice the meat into strips (discard skin), and return to stock. Add coconut milk and simmer.

2 Blend the lemon grass, galingal or ginger, garlic, coriander and chillies. Add this to the stock with the fish sauce, sugar, salt and lime leaves. Simmer for 20 minutes.

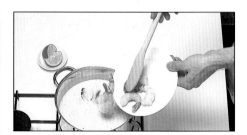

3 Just before serving, add the prawns (shrimp) and lime juice. Simmer for 5 minutes. Decorate with the coriander, spring onions (scallions) and chillies.

DRY BEEF CURRY WITH PEANUT AND LIME

Nua Pad Prik

Dry curries originated from the mountainous northern regions of Thailand but are popular throughout the country. This dry beef curry is usually served with a moist dish such as Ragout of Shellfish with Sweet Scented Basil, or Thai Chicken and Shrimp Soup. The curry is equally delicious made with a lean leg or shoulder of lamb.

SERVES 4–6

Ingredients
2lb stewing beef, (chuck is best), finely chopped
14oz canned coconut milk
1¼ cups beef stock

Red curry paste
2 tbsp coriander seeds
1 tsp cumin seeds
6 green cardamom pods, seeds only
½ tsp ground nutmeg

¼ tsp ground clove
½ tsp ground cinnamon
4 tsp paprika
zest of 1 mandarin orange, finely chopped
4–5 small red chilies, seeded and finely chopped
5 tsp sugar
½ tsp salt
1 piece lemon grass, 4in long, shredded
3 cloves garlic, crushed
1 piece galingal or fresh ginger, ¾in long, peeled and finely chopped
4 red shallots or 1 medium red onion, finely

chopped
1 piece shrimp paste, ¾in square
2oz cilantro, white root or stem, chopped
juice of 2½ limes
2 tbsp vegetable oil
2 tbsp chunky peanut butter
1 lime, sliced, to garnish
1 large red chili, sliced, to garnish
1 small bunch cilantro, shredded, to garnish

1 Place the meat in the freezer for 30–40 minutes until firm. Slice the meat thinly, cut into strips, and chop finely. Strain the coconut milk into a bowl.

2 Place the thin part and half of the thick part of the milk in a large saucepan. Add the beef, and beef stock, bring to a boil, cover, and simmer for 50 minutes.

3 To make the curry paste, dry-fry the coriander, cumin seeds, and cardamom in a wok for 1–2 minutes. Combine with the nutmeg, clove, cinnamon, paprika, and the zest of the mandarin orange. Pound the chilies with the sugar and salt. Add the chili paste, lemon grass, garlic, galingal or ginger, shallots or onion, and shrimp paste. Lastly add the cilantro, juice of ½ lime, and oil.

4 Place a cupful of the cooking liquid in a wok, and add 2–3 tbsp of the curry paste according to taste. Boil rapidly until the liquid has reduced completely. Add the remainder of the coconut milk, the peanut butter, and the beef. Simmer, uncovered, for 15–20 minutes. Stir in the remaining lime juice. Serve decorated with the lime, chili and cilantro.

GREEN CURRY COCONUT CHICKEN

Kaeng Khieu Wan Gai

The recipe given here for green curry paste is a complex one and therefore takes time to make properly. Pork, prawns (shrimp) and fish can all be used instead of chicken, but cooking times must be adjusted accordingly.

SERVES 4–6

Ingredients
1.1kg/2½lb chicken, without giblets
575ml/1 pint/2½ cups canned coconut milk
425ml/¾ pint/1½ cups chicken stock
2 lime leaves

Green curry paste
2 tsp coriander seeds
½ tsp caraway or cumin seeds
3–4 medium green chillies, finely chopped
4 tsp sugar
2 tsp salt
1 piece lemon grass, 7.5cm/3in long
1 piece galingal or fresh ginger, 2cm/¾in long, peeled and finely chopped
3 cloves garlic, crushed
4 shallots or 1 medium onion, finely chopped
1 piece shrimp paste, 2cm/¾in square
3 tbsp coriander leaves, finely chopped
3 tbsp fresh mint or basil, finely chopped
½ tsp nutmeg powder
2 tbsp vegetable oil
350g/12oz sweet potatoes, peeled and roughly chopped
350g/12oz winter squash, peeled, seeded and roughly chopped
115g/4oz French beans, topped, tailed and halved
1 small bunch coriander, shredded, to garnish

1 To prepare the chicken, remove the legs, then separate the thighs from the drumsticks. Separate the lower part of the chicken carcass by cutting through the rib section with kitchen scissors. Divide the breast part in half down the middle, then chop each half in two. Remove skin from all pieces and set aside.

2 Strain the coconut milk into a bowl, reserving the thick part. Place the chicken in a stainless steel or enamel saucepan, cover with the thin part of the coconut milk and the stock. Add the lime leaves, and simmer uncovered for 40 minutes. Remove the chicken from the bone and set aside.

3 Dry-fry the coriander and caraway or cumin seeds. Grind the chillies with the sugar and salt to make a smooth paste. Combine the seeds from the wok with the chillies, the lemon grass, galingal or ginger, garlic and shallots, then grind smoothly. Add the next 5 ingredients.

4 Place a cupful of the cooking liquid in a large wok. Add 4–5 tbsp of the curry paste to the liquid according to taste. Boil rapidly until the liquid has reduced completely. Add the chicken stock, chicken meat, sweet potatoes, squash and beans. Simmer for 10–15 minutes until potatoes are cooked. Just before serving, stir in the thick part of the coconut milk and simmer gently to thicken. Serve decorated with the shredded coriander.

THAI STEAMED FISH WITH A CITRUS MARINADE

Pla Chien

Serve Thai rice or fine rice noodles as an accompaniment to this dish.

SERVES 4–6

Ingredients
1.3kg/3lb parrot fish, pomfret, plaice or sea
    bream, gutted with heads on
2 small red chillies, seeded and finely
    chopped
1 tbsp sugar
2 cloves garlic, crushed
3 spring onions (scallions), white part only,
    chopped
1 piece fresh galingal or fresh ginger, 2.5cm/1in
    long, peeled and finely chopped
juice of 1 mandarin orange
zest of 1 mandarin orange, finely chopped
1 tbsp tamarind sauce
1 tbsp fish sauce
2 tbsp light soy sauce
juice of 1 lime
1 tbsp vegetable oil
2 limes, quartered, to garnish
4 spring onion (scallion) curls, to garnish

1 Wash the fish thoroughly and slash 3–4 times with a sharp knife on each side to allow the marinade to penetrate deeply. Place the fish in a shallow dish that will fit in the base of a steamer. You can also wrap the fish loosely in foil.

2 Grind the chilli and sugar together using a pestle and mortar or food processor, add the garlic, spring onion (scallion), galingal or ginger and the zest of the mandarin orange. Combine well. Lastly add the tamarind, fish and soy sauces, the lime juice and vegetable oil, then spread over the fish. Leave to marinate for at least 1 hour.

3 Cook the fish in a covered steamer for 25–30 minutes. Lift the fish onto a serving plate and decorate with wedges of lime and spring onion (scallion).

PORK AND PEANUT PICK-ME-UPS

Ma Hor

With a Thai meal, it is not customary to have a starter. Instead, appetizers are served with drinks beforehand.

MAKES 12

Ingredients
1 tbsp vegetable oil
2 shallots, or 1 small onion, finely chopped
1 clove garlic, crushed
1 piece fresh ginger, 2cm/¾in long, peeled and
    finely chopped

1 small red chilli, seeded and finely chopped
150g/5oz minced (ground) pork, or the contents
    of 150g/5oz fresh pork sausages
2 tbsp peanut butter
1 tbsp fish sauce
juice of ½ lime
4 tsp sugar
2 tbsp chopped coriander leaves

4 clementines, peeled and thickly sliced
6 ramboutans, or lychees, peeled and stoned
    (pitted)
1 small pineapple, peeled, cored and sliced
1 firm pear, peeled, cored and sliced
1 lime, cut into small wedges, to garnish
12 coriander leaves, to garnish

1 Heat the oil and fry the next 4 ingredients. Add the pork and cook for 10 minutes.

2 Add the peanut butter, fish sauce, lime juice, sugar and chopped coriander.

3 Spoon the topping onto pieces of fruit. Decorate with lime and coriander leaves.

THAI DIPPING SAUCE

Nam Prik

Nam Prik is the most common dipping sauce in Thailand. It has a fiery strength, so use with caution.

MAKES 120ML/4 FL OZ/½ CUP

Ingredients
1 tbsp vegetable oil
1 piece shrimp paste, 12mm/½in square,
   or 1 tbsp fish sauce
2 cloves garlic, finely sliced
1 piece fresh ginger, 2cm/¾in long, peeled and
   finely chopped
3 small red chillies, seeded and chopped
1 tbsp finely-chopped coriander root or stem
4 tsp sugar
3 tbsp dark soy sauce
juice of ½ lime

1 Heat the vegetable oil in a wok, add the shrimp paste or fish sauce, garlic, ginger and chillies and soften without colouring, for about 1–2 minutes.

2 Remove from the heat and add the coriander, sugar, soy sauce and lime juice. Nam Prik Sauce will keep in a screw-top jar for up to 10 days.

HOT COCONUT PRAWN (SHRIMP) AND PAW PAW SALAD

Yam Ma-La-Kaw Prik

This dish may be served as an accompaniment to beef and chicken dishes.

SERVES 4–6

Ingredients
225g/8oz fresh or cooked prawn (shrimp) tails,
   peeled and de-veined
2 ripe paw paws, or papayas
225g/8oz cos, iceberg or bib lettuce leaves,
   Chinese leaves and young spinach

1 firm tomato, skinned, seeded and roughly
   chopped
3 spring onions (scallions), shredded

Dressing
1 tbsp creamed coconut
2 tbsp boiling water
6 tbsp vegetable oil

juice of 1 lime
½ tsp hot chilli sauce
2 tsp fish sauce (optional)
1 tsp sugar
1 small bunch coriander, shredded, to garnish
1 large chilli, sliced, to garnish

1 To make the dressing, place the creamed coconut in a screw-top jar and add the boiling water to soften. Add the vegetable oil, lime juice, chilli sauce, fish sauce if using and sugar. Shake well and set aside. Do not refrigerate.

2 If using fresh prawn (shrimp) tails, cover with cold water in a saucepan, bring to the boil and simmer for no longer than 2 minutes. Drain and set aside.

3 To prepare the paw paws or papayas, cut each in half from top to bottom and remove the black seeds with a teaspoon. Peel away the outer skin and cut the flesh into even-sized pieces. Wash the salad leaves and toss in a bowl. Add the other ingredients. Pour on the dressing and serve.

RED CURRY BEEF WITH TAMARIND

Kang Mussaman Nuea

This red curry can also be made using diced lamb, in which case reduce the cooking time by 30 minutes.

SERVES 4–6

Ingredients
900g/2lb stewing (braising), chuck, shin or blade steak
400g/14oz canned coconut milk
300ml/½ pint/1¼ cups beef stock

Red curry paste
2 tbsp coriander seeds
1 tsp cumin seeds
6 green cardamom pods, seeds only
½ tsp nutmeg powder
¼ tsp clove powder
½ tsp cinnamon powder
4 tsp paprika
zest of 1 mandarin orange, finely chopped
4–5 small red chillies, seeded and finely chopped
5 tsp sugar
½ tsp salt
1 piece lemon grass, 10cm/4in long, shredded
3 cloves garlic, crushed
1 piece galingal or fresh ginger, 2cm/¾in long, peeled and finely chopped
4 red shallots or 1 medium red onion, finely chopped
1 piece shrimp paste, 2cm/¾in square
50g/2oz coriander, white root or stem, chopped
2 tbsp vegetable oil
350g/12oz new potatoes, peeled and roughly chopped
350g/12oz pumpkin or winter squash
200g/7oz canned bamboo shoots, sliced
2 tbsp smooth peanut butter
2 tbsp tamarind sauce
juice of 2 limes
1 small bunch coriander, to garnish

1 Cut the beef into 2.5cm/1in dice and place in a stainless steel saucepan.

2 Place the coconut milk in a fine sieve and allow the thin part of the milk to drain into a bowl. Add all the thin and half of the thick part of the coconut milk to the saucepan. Add the stock, bring to the boil and simmer uncovered for 1 hour. Strain and set aside.

3 Dry-fry the coriander, cumin seeds and cardamom in a wok for 1–2 minutes. Combine with the nutmeg, clove, cinnamon, paprika and mandarin zest, and grind. Pound the chillies with the sugar and salt. Add the chilli paste, lemon grass, garlic, galingal, shallots and shrimp paste. Add the coriander and oil and reduce.

4 Place a cupful of the cooking liquid in a large wok. Add 2–3 tbsp of the paste. Boil rapidly to reduce the liquid. Add the peanut butter and tamarind sauce. Add the beef, potatoes, pumpkin and bamboo shoots and simmer for 20–25 minutes until the potatoes are cooked. Stir in the thick part of the coconut milk and the lime juice. Return to a gentle simmer. Decorate, and serve with Thai rice.

COCONUT MILK

Coconut milk is used to enrich and flavour many dishes in the Far East. Only the Japanese choose not to include it in their cooking. Coconut milk is not, as many suppose, the liquid found inside the nut. Although this thin liquid does make a refreshing drink, the coconut milk used for cooking is processed from the white flesh of the nut. If left to stand, the thick part of the milk will rise to the surface like cream. If the milk is cold the thick part of the milk will separate more easily. Choose a coconut with plenty of milk inside. Shake the nut firmly. If you cannot hear the milk sloshing around, the flesh will be difficult to remove. If you can find a coconut with its green husk and fibre attached, the flesh will almost certainly be soft and creamy white. Fresh coconut milk will keep in a cool place for up to 10 days. If kept in the refrigerator, allow to soften at room temperature before using.

MAKES 400ml/14fl oz/1¾ cups

Ingredients
2 fresh coconuts
1.1 litres/2 pints/5 cups water, off the boil

1 Hold the coconut over a bowl to collect the liquid. With the back of a large knife or cleaver, crack open the coconut by striking it cleanly.

2 Scrape out the white meat with a citrus zester or a rounded butter curler. Place the coconut meat in a food processor with half of the water.

3 Process for 1 minute, then pass through a food mill or mouli fitted with a fine disk, catching the milk in a bowl beneath. Alternatively, squeeze the coconut meat with your hands and press through a nylon strainer. Return the coconut meat to the food processor or mill with the remainder of the water, blend and press for a second time. Allow the milk to settle for 30 minutes (creamy solids will rise to the surface). Sometimes the solids should be poured off and added later as a thickener.

Cook's tip

Coconut milk can be obtained directly from coconut flesh – this gives the creamiest milk; from a can – which may be expensive; as a soluble powder and as creamed coconut which is sold in block form. Powder and creamed coconut make a poor milk, but are useful additions to sauces and dressings.

RAGOUT OF SHELLFISH WITH SWEET SCENTED BASIL

Po-Tak

Green curry paste can be used to accompany other dishes, such as Green Curry Coconut Chicken. Curry pastes will keep for up to 3 weeks in the refrigerator if stored in a screw-top jar.

SERVES 4–6

Ingredients

575ml/1 pint/2½ cups fresh mussels in their shells, cleaned
225g/8oz medium cuttle fish or squid
350g/12oz monkfish, hokey or red snapper, skinned
150g/5oz fresh or cooked prawn (shrimp) tails, peeled and de-veined
4 scallops, sliced (optional)
400ml/14oz canned coconut milk
300ml/½ pint/1¼ cups chicken or vegetable stock
85g/3oz French beans, trimmed and cooked

50g/2oz canned bamboo shoots, drained
1 ripe tomato, skinned, seeded and roughly chopped

Green curry paste
2 tsp coriander seeds
½ tsp caraway or cumin seeds
3–4 medium green chillies, finely chopped
4 tsp sugar
2 tsp salt
1 piece lemon grass, 7.5cm/3in long
1 piece galingal or fresh ginger, 2cm/¾in long, peeled and finely chopped
3 cloves garlic, crushed
4 shallots or 1 medium onion, finely chopped

1 piece shrimp paste, 2cm/¾in square
50g/2oz coriander leaves, finely chopped
3 tbsp fresh mint or basil, finely chopped
½ tsp nutmeg
2 tbsp vegetable oil
4 sprigs large leaf basil, torn, to garnish

1 Place the mussels in a stainless steel or enamel saucepan, add 4 tbsp of water, cover, steam open and cook for 6–8 minutes. Take ¾ of the mussels out of their shells (discard any which don't open), strain the cooking liquid and set aside.

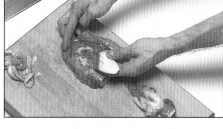

2 To prepare the cuttle fish or squid, trim off the tentacles beneath the eye. Rinse under cold running water, discarding the gut. Remove the cuttle shell from inside the body and rub off the paper-thin skin. Cut the body open and score, criss-cross, with a sharp knife. Cut into strips and set aside.

3 To make the green curry paste, dry-fry the coriander and caraway or cumin seeds in a wok to release their flavour. Grind the chillies with the sugar and salt using a pestle and mortar or food processor to make a smooth paste. Combine the seeds from the wok with the chillies, add the lemon grass, galingal or ginger, garlic and shallots or onion, then grind smoothly. Add the shrimp paste, coriander, mint or basil, nutmeg and vegetable oil. Combine well. There may seem to be a lot of coriander and mint at this stage, but their volume will reduce considerably when ground with the other spices.

4 Pour the coconut milk into a sieve. Pour the thin part of the milk together with the chicken or vegetable stock into a wok. The thick part of the coconut milk is added later. Add 4–5 tbsp of the green curry paste according to taste. You can add more paste later if you need to. Boil rapidly until the liquid has reduced completely.

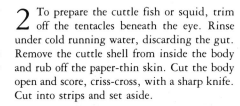

5 Add the thick part of the coconut milk, then add the cuttle fish or squid and monkfish, hokey or red snapper. Simmer uncovered for 15–20 minutes. Then add the prawns (shrimp), scallops and cooked mussels with the beans, bamboo shoots and tomato. Simmer for 2–3 minutes, transfer to a bowl and decorate with the basil and chillies.

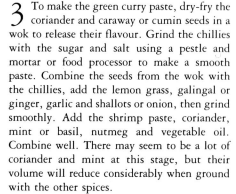

BRAISED WHOLE FISH IN CHILLI AND GARLIC SAUCE

Gan Shao Yu

This recipe reflects its Chinese origins. When served in a restaurant, the fish's head and tail are usually discarded before cooking, and used in other dishes. A whole fish may be used, however, and always looks impressive, especially for formal occasions and dinner parties.

SERVES 4–6

Ingredients

1 carp, bream, sea bass, trout, grouper or grey mullet, weighing about 675g/1½lb, gutted
1 tbsp light soy sauce
1 tbsp rice wine or dry sherry
vegetable oil, for deep-frying

Sauce

2 cloves garlic, finely chopped
2–3 spring onions (scallions), finely chopped with the white and green parts separated
1 tsp finely-chopped fresh ginger
2 tbsp chilli bean sauce
1 tbsp tomato purée (paste)
2 tsp light brown sugar
1 tbsp rice vinegar
about 100ml/4fl oz/½ cup stock
1 tbsp cornflour (cornstarch) paste
few drops sesame oil

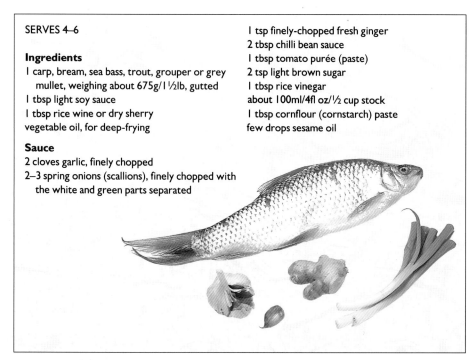

1 Rinse and dry the fish well. Using a sharp knife, score both sides of the fish as far down as the bone with diagonal cuts about 2.5cm/1in apart. Rub the whole fish with soy sauce and wine or sherry on both sides, then leave to marinate for 10–15 minutes.

2 In a wok, deep-fry the fish in hot oil for about 3–4 minutes on both sides or until golden brown.

3 Pour off the excess oil, leaving about 1 tbsp in the wok. Push the fish to one side of the wok and add the garlic, the white part of the spring onions (scallions), ginger, chilli bean sauce, tomato purée (paste), sugar, vinegar and stock. Bring to the boil and braise the fish in the sauce for 4–5 minutes, turning it over once. Add the green part of the spring onions (scallions). Thicken the sauce with the cornflour (cornstarch) paste, sprinkle with the sesame oil and serve.

STEAMED FISH WITH GINGER AND SPRING ONIONS (SCALLIONS)

Qing Zheng Yu

Any firm and delicate fish steaks, such as salmon or turbot, can be cooked by this same method.

SERVES 4–6

Ingredients
1 sea bass, trout or grey mullet, weighing
    about 675g/1½lb, gutted
½ tsp salt
1 tbsp sesame oil

2–3 spring onions (scallions), cut in half lengthways
2 tbsp light soy sauce
2 tbsp rice wine or dry sherry
1 tbsp finely-shredded fresh ginger
2 tbsp vegetable oil
finely-shredded spring onions (scallions), to
    garnish

1 Using a sharp knife, score both sides of the fish as far down as the bone with diagonal cuts about 2.5cm/1in apart. Rub the fish all over, inside and out, with salt and sesame oil.

2 Sprinkle the spring onions (scallions) on a heatproof platter and place the fish on top. Blend together the soy sauce and wine or sherry with the ginger shreds and pour evenly all over the fish.

3 Place the platter in a very hot steamer (or inside a wok on a rack), and steam vigorously, under cover, for 12–15 minutes.

4 Heat the oil until hot; remove the platter from the steamer, place the shredded spring onions (scallions) on top of the fish, then pour the hot oil along the whole length of the fish. Serve immediately.

RED AND WHITE PRAWNS (SHRIMP) WITH GREEN VEGETABLES

Yuan Yang Xia

Rice and salad are the ideal accompaniments to this Chinese-influenced recipe. The name of the dish is similar in meaning to 'love birds', symbolizing affection and happiness.

SERVES 4–6

Ingredients
450g/1lb uncooked prawns (shrimp)
pinch of salt
½ egg white
1 tbsp cornflour (cornstarch) paste
175g/6oz mange-tout (snow peas)
about 575ml/1 pint/2½ cups vegetable oil
½ tsp salt

1 tsp light brown sugar
1 tbsp finely-chopped spring onions (scallions)
1 tsp finely-chopped fresh ginger
1 tbsp light soy sauce
1 tbsp rice wine or dry sherry
1 tsp chilli bean sauce
1 tbsp tomato purée (paste)

1 Peel and de-vein the prawns (shrimp), and mix with the pinch of salt, the egg white and the cornflour (cornstarch) paste. Top and tail the mange-tout (snow peas).

2 Heat about 2–3 tbsp of the oil in a preheated wok and stir-fry the mange-tout (snow peas) for about 1 minute, then add the salt and sugar and continue stirring for another minute. Remove and place in the centre of a serving platter.

3 Heat the remaining oil, par-cook the prawns (shrimp) for 1 minute, remove and drain.

4 Pour off the excess oil, leaving about 1 tbsp in the wok, and add the spring onions (scallions) and ginger to flavour the oil.

5 Add the prawns (shrimp) and stir-fry for about 1 minute, then add the soy sauce and wine or sherry. Blend well and place about half of the prawns (shrimp) at one end of the platter.

6 Add the chilli bean sauce and tomato purée (paste) to the remaining prawns (shrimp) in the wok, blend well and place the 'red' prawns (shrimp) at the other end of the platter. Serve.

PRAWNS (SHRIMP) COOKED WITH OKRA

Jingha Aur Bhendi

This dish has a sweet taste with a strong chilli flavour. It should be cooked fast to prevent the okra from breaking up and releasing its distinctive, sticky interior.

SERVES 4–6	I piece fresh ginger, 5cm/2in long, crushed	de-veined
	4–6 green chillies, cut diagonally	salt, to taste
Ingredients	½ tsp turmeric	2 tsp brown sugar
4–6 tbsp oil	4–6 curry leaves	juice of 2 lemons
225g/8oz okra, washed, dried and left whole	I tsp cumin seeds	
4 cloves garlic, crushed	450g/1lb fresh king prawns (shrimp), peeled and	

1 Heat the oil in a frying pan and fry the okra on a fairly high heat until they are slightly crisp and browned on all sides. Remove from the oil and keep aside on a piece of kitchen paper.

2 In the same oil, gently fry the garlic, ginger, chillies, turmeric, curry leaves and cumin seeds for 2–3 minutes. Add the prawns (shrimp) and mix well. Cook until the prawns (shrimp) are tender.

3 Add the salt, sugar, lemon juice and fried okra. Increase the heat and quickly fry for a further 5 minutes, stirring gently to prevent the okra from breaking. Adjust the seasoning, if necessary. Serve hot.

FRIED WHOLE FISH

Tali Huvey Macchi

Rice and a dipping sauce are the perfect table partners to this dish which has origins that can be traced back to the shores of Southern India.

SERVES 4–6

Ingredients
I small onion, coarsely chopped
4 cloves garlic, peeled
I piece fresh ginger, 5cm/2in long, peeled
I tsp turmeric
2 tsp chilli powder
salt, to taste
4 red mullets
vegetable oil, for shallow-frying
I tsp cumin seeds
3 green chillies, finely sliced
lemon wedges, to serve

1 Using a food processor, grind the first 6 ingredients to a smooth paste. Make gashes on both sides of the fish and rub them with the paste. Leave to rest for 1 hour. Lightly pat the fish dry with kitchen paper without removing the paste. Excess fluid will be released as the salt dissolves.

2 Heat the oil in a large frying pan and fry the cumin seeds and chillies for about 1 minute. Add the fish and fry on one side without overlapping. When the first side is sealed, turn the fish over very gently to ensure they do not break. Fry until they are golden brown on both sides, drain well and serve hot with lemon or lime wedges.

THAI FRUIT AND VEGETABLE SALAD

Yam Chomphu

This fruit salad is presented with the main course and serves as a cooler to counteract the heat of the chillies.

SERVES 4–6

Ingredients
1 small pineapple
1 small mango, peeled and sliced
1 green apple, cored and sliced
6 ramboutans or lychees, peeled and stoned (pitted)
115g/4oz French beans, topped, tailed and halved
1 medium red onion, sliced
1 small cucumber, cut into short fingers

115g/4oz bean sprouts
2 spring onions (scallions), sliced
1 ripe tomato, quartered
225g/8oz cos, bib or iceberg lettuce leaves

Coconut dipping sauce
6 tsp coconut cream
2 tbsp sugar
5 tbsp boiling water
¼ tsp chilli sauce
1 tbsp fish sauce
juice of 1 lime

Cook's tip

Creamed coconut is sold in 200g/7oz blocks and is available from large supermarkets and specialist food stores. In warm weather, creamed coconut should be stored in a cool place to keep it from softening.

1 To make the coconut dipping sauce, measure the coconut, sugar and boiling water into a screw-top jar. Add the chilli and fish sauces and lime juice and shake.

2 Trim both ends of the pineapple with a serrated knife, then cut away the outer skin. Remove the central core with an apple corer. Alternatively, cut the pineapple into 4 down the middle and remove the core with a knife. Roughly chop the pineapple and set aside with the other fruits.

3 Bring a small saucepan of salted water to the boil and cook the beans for 3–4 minutes. Refresh under cold running water and set aside. To serve, arrange the fruits and vegetables into small heaps on a shallow bowl. Serve the coconut sauce separately as a dip.

SWEET CUCUMBER COOLER

Ajad

Sweet dipping sauces such as this bring instant relief to the hot chilli flavours of Thai food.

MAKES 120ML/4 FL OZ/½ CUP

Ingredients
5 tbsp water
2 tbsp sugar
½ tsp salt
1 tbsp rice or white wine vinegar
¼ small cucumber, quartered and thinly sliced
2 shallots, or 1 small red onion, thinly sliced

1 Measure the water, sugar, salt and vinegar into a stainless steel or enamel saucepan, bring to the boil and simmer until the sugar has dissolved, for less than 1 minute.

2 Allow to cool. Add the cucumber and shallots or onion and serve at room temperature.

HONEY-GLAZED QUAIL WITH A FIVE-SPICE MARINADE

Bo Can Quay

Chinese supermarkets sell five-spice powder in packets. Provided the blend is not kept for longer than 3 months, the flavour can be good, and a useful alternative to making your own.

SERVES 4–6

Ingredients
4 quails, cleaned
2 pieces star anise
2 tsp cinnamon powder
2 tsp fennel seeds
2 tsp Sichuan, or Chinese pepper
a pinch powdered cloves
1 small onion, finely chopped

1 clove garlic, crushed
4 tbsp clear honey
2 tbsp dark soy sauce
2 roughly chopped spring onions (scallions), to garnish
mandarin orange or satsuma, to garnish
banana leaves, to serve

1 Remove the backbones from the quails by cutting down either side with a pair of kitchen scissors.

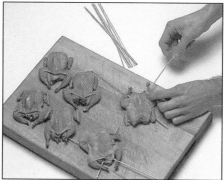

2 Flatten the birds with the palm of your hand and secure each bird using 2 bamboo skewers.

3 Place the five spices in a pestle and mortar or spice mill and grind into a fine powder. Add the onion, garlic, honey and soy sauce, and combine well.

4 Place the quails in a flat dish, cover with the marinade and leave for at least 8 hours for the flavours to mingle.

5 Preheat a grill or barbecue to a moderate temperature and cook the quails for 7–8 minutes on each side, basting occasionally with the marinade.

6 To garnish, remove the outer zest from the mandarin orange or satsuma with a vegetable peeler or a zesting tool. Shred the zest finely and combine with the chopped spring onions (scallions). Arrange the quails on a bed of banana leaves, garnish with the orange zest and spring onions (scallions) and serve.

HOT CHILLI CHICKEN WITH GINGER AND LEMON GRASS

Ga Xao Xa Ot

This dish can also be prepared using duck legs. Be sure to remove the jointed parts of the drumsticks and thigh bones to make the meat easier to eat with chopsticks.

SERVES 4–6

Ingredients
3 chicken legs (thighs and drumsticks)
I tbsp vegetable oil
I piece fresh ginger, 2cm/¾in long, peeled and finely chopped

I clove garlic, crushed
I small red chilli, seeded and finely chopped
I piece lemon grass, 5cm/2in long, shredded
I50ml/¼ pint/⅔ cup chicken stock
I tbsp fish sauce (optional)
2 tsp sugar
½ tsp salt

juice of ½ lemon
50g/2oz raw peanuts
2 spring onions (scallions), shredded
I zest of mandarin orange or satsuma, shredded
2 tbsp chopped mint
rice or rice noodles, to serve

1 With the heel of the knife, chop through the narrow end of the drumsticks. Remove the jointed parts of the drumsticks and thigh bones, then remove the skin.

2 Heat the oil in a large wok or frying pan. Add the chicken, ginger, garlic, chilli and lemon grass and cook for 3–4 minutes. Add the chicken stock, fish sauce if using, sugar, salt and lemon juice. Cover and simmer for 30–35 minutes.

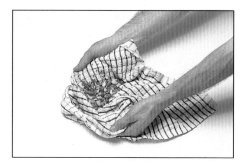

3 To prepare the peanuts for the topping, the red skin must be removed. To do this, grill (broil) or roast the peanuts under a steady heat until evenly brown, for about 2–3 minutes. Turn the nuts out onto a clean cloth and rub briskly to loosen the skins.

4 Serve the chicken scattered with roasted peanuts, shredded spring onions (scallions) and the zest of the mandarin orange or satsuma. Serve with rice or rice noodles.

CRAB, PORK AND MUSHROOM SPRING ROLLS

Cha Gio

If you cannot obtain minced (ground) pork, use the meat from the equivalent weight of best-quality pork sausages. Filled spring rolls can be made in advance and kept in the refrigerator ready for frying.

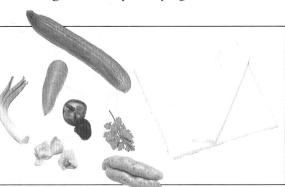

MAKES 12 ROLLS

Ingredients
25g/1oz rice noodles
50g/2oz Chinese mushrooms (shiitake), fresh or dried
1 tbsp vegetable oil
4 spring onions (scallions), chopped
1 small carrot, grated
175g/6oz minced (ground) pork

100g/4oz/1 cup white crabmeat
1 tsp fish sauce (optional)
salt and pepper
12 frozen spring roll skins, defrosted
2 tbsp cornflour (cornstarch) paste
vegetable oil, for deep-frying
1 head iceberg or bib lettuce, to serve
1 bunch mint or basil, to serve
1 bunch coriander leaves, to serve
½ cucumber, sliced, to serve

1 Bring a large saucepan of salted water to the boil, and simmer the noodles for 8 minutes. Cut the noodles into finger-length pieces. If the mushrooms are dried, soak them in boiling water for 10 minutes before slicing thinly.

2 To make the filling, heat the oil in a wok or frying pan, add the spring onions (scallions), carrot and pork and cook for 8–10 minutes. Remove from the heat, then add the crabmeat, fish sauce and seasoning. Add the noodles and mushrooms, and set aside.

3 To fill the rolls, brush one spring roll skin at a time with the cornflour (cornstarch) paste, then place 1 tsp of the filling onto the skin. Fold the edges towards the middle and roll evenly to make a neat cigar shape. The paste will help seal the wrapper.

4 Heat the oil in a wok or deep-fryer until hot. Fry the spring rolls two at a time in the oil for 6–8 minutes. Make sure the fat is not too hot or the mixture inside will not heat through properly. Serve on a bed of salad leaves, mint, coriander and cucumber.

HOT AND SOUR CHICKEN SALAD

Ga Nuong Ngu Vi

This salad is also delicious with prawns (shrimp). Allow 450g/1lb of fresh prawn (shrimp) tails to serve 4.

SERVES 4–6

Ingredients
2 chicken breast fillets, skinned
1 small red chilli, seeded and finely chopped
1 piece fresh ginger, 12mm/½in long, peeled and finely chopped

1 clove garlic, crushed
1 tbsp crunchy peanut butter
2 tbsp chopped coriander leaves
1 tsp sugar
½ tsp salt
1 tbsp rice or white wine vinegar
4 tbsp vegetable oil

2 tsp fish sauce (optional)
115g/4oz bean sprouts
1 head Chinese leaves, roughly shredded
2 medium carrots, cut into thin sticks
1 red onion, cut into fine rings
2 large gherkins (pickles), sliced

1 Slice the chicken thinly, place in a shallow bowl and set aside. Grind the chilli, ginger and garlic in a pestle and mortar. Add the peanut butter, coriander, sugar and salt.

2 Then add the vinegar, 2 tbsp of the oil and the fish sauce if using. Combine well. Cover the chicken with the spice mixture and leave to marinate for at least 2–3 hours.

3 Heat the remaining 2 tbsp of oil in a wok or frying pan. Add the chicken and cook for 10–12 minutes, tossing the meat occasionally. Serve arranged on the salad.

ALFALFA CRAB SALAD WITH CRISPY FRIED NOODLES

Goi Gia

Alfalfa sprouts are available in many supermarkets. Alternatively, you can grow your own sprouts from seeds.

SERVES 4–6

Ingredients
vegetable oil, for deep-frying
50g/2oz Chinese rice noodles, uncooked
2 dressed crabs, or 150g/5oz frozen white crab meat, thawed
115g/4oz alfalfa sprouts

1 small iceberg or bib lettuce
4 sprigs coriander, roughly chopped
1 ripe tomato, skinned, seeded and diced
4 sprigs fresh mint, roughly chopped

Sesame lime dressing
3 tbsp vegetable oil
1 tsp sesame oil

½ small red chilli, seeded and finely chopped
1 piece stem ginger in syrup, cut into matchsticks
2 tsp stem ginger syrup
2 tsp soy sauce
juice of ½ lime

1 Combine the vegetable and sesame oils in a bowl. Add the chilli, stem ginger, stem ginger syrup and soy sauce with the lime juice.

2 Heat the oil in a deep-fryer to 196°C/385°F. Fry the noodles, one handful at a time, until crisp. Lift out and dry on paper.

3 Flake the white crab meat into a bowl and toss with the alfalfa sprouts. Serve on a nest of noodles and tossed salad ingredients.

PORK BALLS WITH A MINTED PEANUT SAUCE

Nem Nuong

This recipe is equally delicious made with chicken breasts.

SERVES 4–6

Ingredients
285g/10oz leg of pork, trimmed
    and diced
1 piece fresh ginger, 12mm/½in long,
    peeled and grated
1 clove garlic, crushed
2 tsp sesame oil
1 tbsp medium-dry sherry
1 tbsp soy sauce

1 tsp sugar
1 egg white
½ tsp salt
a pinch of white pepper
350g/12oz long grain rice, washed and
    cooked for 15 minutes
50g/2oz ham, thickly sliced and diced
1 iceberg or bib lettuce, to serve

Minted peanut sauce
1 tbsp creamed coconut
75ml/5 tbsp/⅓ cup boiling water
2 tbsp smooth peanut butter
juice of 1 lime
1 red chilli, seeded and finely chopped
1 clove garlic, crushed
1 tbsp freshly-chopped mint
1 tbsp freshly-chopped coriander
1 tbsp fish sauce (optional)

1 To make the pork balls, place the diced pork, ginger and garlic in a food processor and blend together smoothly for about 2–3 minutes. Add the sesame oil, sherry, soy sauce and sugar and blend. Lastly add the egg white.

2 Spread the cooked rice and ham on a shallow dish. Using wet hands, shape the pork mixture into thumb-sized balls. Roll in the rice to cover and pierce each ball with a bamboo skewer.

3 To make the sauce, put the creamed coconut in a measuring jug and cover with the boiling water. Place the peanut butter in another bowl with the lime juice, chilli, garlic, mint and coriander. Combine evenly, then add the creamed coconut and season with the fish sauce if using.

4 Place the pork balls in a bamboo steamer, cover and steam over a saucepan of boiling water for 8–10 minutes. Arrange all the lettuce leaves on a large serving plate. Place the pork balls on the leaves with the dipping sauce to one side.

EXOTIC FRUIT SALAD

Hoa Qua Tron

A variety of fruits can be used for this salad depending on what is available. Look out for mandarin oranges, star fruit, paw paw, Cape gooseberries and passion fruit.

SERVES 4–6

Ingredients
85g/3oz/6tbsp sugar
300ml/½ pint/1¼ cups water
2 tbsp stem ginger syrup
2 pieces star anise
1 piece cinnamon stick, 2.5cm/1 in long
1 clove
juice of ½ lemon
2 sprigs mint

1 medium pineapple
1 mango, peeled and sliced
2 bananas, sliced
8 lychees, fresh or canned
225g/8oz fresh strawberries, trimmed and halved
2 pieces stem ginger, cut into sticks

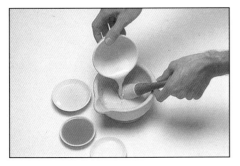

1 Measure the sugar into a saucepan, and add the water, ginger syrup, spices, lemon juice and mint. Bring to the boil and simmer for 3 minutes. Strain into a large bowl and allow to cool.

2 Remove both the top and bottom from the mango and remove the outer skin. Stand the mango on one end and remove the flesh in two pieces either side of the flat stone (pit). Slice evenly and add to the syrup. Add the bananas, lychees, strawberries and ginger. Chill until ready to serve.

3 Cut the pineapple in half down the centre. Loosen the flesh with a small serrated knife and remove to form two boat shapes. Cut the flesh into large chunks and place in the cooled syrup.

4 Spoon the fruit salad into the pineapple halves and bring to the table on a large serving dish. There will be enough fruit salad left over to refill the pineapple halves.

PORK AND NOODLE BROTH WITH PRAWNS (SHRIMP)

Pho

This quick and delicious recipe can be made with 200g/7oz boneless chicken breast instead of pork fillet.

SERVES 4–6

Ingredients
350g/12oz pork chops or 200g/7oz pork fillet
225g/8oz fresh prawn (shrimp) tails or cooked
    prawns (shrimp)
150g/5oz thin egg noodles
1 tbsp vegetable oil
2 tsp sesame oil
4 shallots, or 1 medium onion, sliced
1 tbsp fresh ginger, finely sliced

1 clove garlic, crushed
1 tsp granulated sugar
1.4 litres/2½ pints/6¼ cups chicken stock
2 lime leaves
3 tbsp fish sauce
juice of ½ lime
4 sprigs coriander leaves, to garnish
chopped green part of 2 spring onions (scallions),
    to garnish

1 If using pork chops, trim away fat and bone completely. Place the meat in the freezer for 30 minutes to firm but not freeze the meat. Slice the meat thinly and set aside. Peel and de-vein the prawns (shrimp), if fresh.

2 Bring a large saucepan of salted water to the boil and simmer the noodles for the time stated on the packet. Drain and refresh under cold running water. Set aside.

3 Heat the vegetable and sesame oils in a large saucepan, add the shallots and brown evenly, for 3–4 minutes. Remove from the pan and set aside.

4 Add the ginger, garlic, sugar and chicken stock and bring to a simmer with the lime leaves. Add the fish sauce and lime juice. Add the pork, then simmer for 15 minutes. Add the prawns and noodles and simmer for 3–4 minutes. Serve in shallow soup bowls and decorate with the coriander leaves, the green part of the spring onions (scallions) and the browned shallots.

VIETNAMESE DIPPING SAUCE

Nuoc Cham

Serve this dip in a small bowl as an accompaniment to spring rolls or meat dishes.

MAKES 150ML/5 FL OZ/⅔ CUP

Ingredients
1–2 small red chillies, seeded and finely chopped
1 clove garlic, crushed
1 tbsp roasted peanuts
4 tbsp coconut milk
2 tbsp fish sauce
juice of 1 lime
2 tsp sugar
1 tsp chopped coriander leaves

1 Crush the red chilli together with the garlic and peanuts using a pestle and mortar or food processor.

2 Add the coconut milk, fish sauce, lime juice, sugar and coriander.

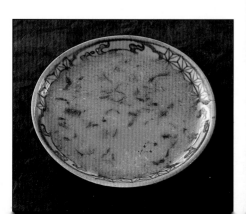

HANDLING CHILLIES

Chillies are an important part of Eastern cookery and should be handled with care. The pungent oils released when chillies are cut can be harmful to sensitive parts of the skin, especially to eyes and lips. Be sure to wash your hands thoroughly with soap and water after touching cut chillies.

1 The severe heat of red and green chillies is contained in the seeds. Unless you like fiercely hot food, the seeds should be discarded before using. It is most practical to wash the seeds away under cold running water.

2 A useful chilli flavouring can be made by storing chillies in a jar of oil. Allow the hot flavours to merge for 3 weeks before using. Chilli oil is used to add a gentle heat to many Eastern dishes.

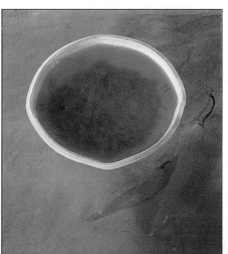

CUCUMBER AND CARROT GARNISHES

Presentation is an important part of South-east Asian cooking. These vegetable decorations are easily prepared.

MAKES 2 DECORATIVE GARNISHES

Ingredients
½ cucumber
1 large carrot

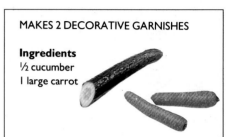

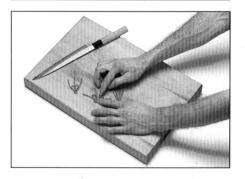

1 To make the cucumber garnish, cut the cucumber into a 7.5cm/3in strip, 2cm/¾in wide. Make 5 even cuts along the strip, 12mm/½in in from one end. Curl the second and fourth strips towards the base to form an open loop. The same cucumber strip can be spread out to form an attractive fan shape.

2 To make the carrot garnish, peel the carrot and cut into 6mm/¼in slices. Trim the slices into rectangles, 2cm/¾in × 7.5cm/3in. Make a 6mm/¼in cut along one edge of the carrot so that the strip is still joined. Make a second cut in the other direction, again so that the strip is joined. Bend the two ends together so that they cross over. This garnish can also be fashioned with giant white radish, cucumber and lemon peel.

MAIN COURSE SPICY PRAWN (SHRIMP) AND NOODLE SOUP

Laksa Lemak

This dish is served as a hot coconut broth with a separate platter of prawns (shrimp), fish and noodles. Diners are invited to add their own choice of accompaniment to the broth.

SERVES 4–6

Ingredients
25g/1oz raw cashew nuts
3 shallots, or 1 medium onion, sliced
1 piece lemon grass, 5cm/2in long, shredded
2 cloves garlic, crushed
2 tbsp vegetable oil
1 piece shrimp paste, 12mm/½in square,
   or 1 tbsp fish sauce
1 tbsp mild curry paste
400g/14oz canned coconut milk
½ chicken stock cube
3 curry leaves (optional)
450g/1lb white fish fillet, cod, haddock or whiting
225g/8oz prawn (shrimp) tails, fresh or cooked
1 small cos lettuce, shredded
115g/4oz bean sprouts
3 spring onions (scallions), shredded
½ cucumber, sliced and shredded
150g/5oz Laksa noodles (spaghetti-size rice
   noodles), soaked for 10 minutes before cooking
Prawn Crackers, to serve

Cook's tip

To serve, line a large serving platter with the shredded lettuce leaves. Arrange the salad ingredients in neat piles together with the cooked fish, prawns (shrimp) and noodles. Serve the salad with a bowl of Prawn Crackers and the broth in a stoneware closed-rim pot.

1 Grind the cashew nuts using a pestle and mortar or food processor with the shallots or onion, lemon grass and garlic. Cook the noodles according to the instructions.

2 Heat the oil in a large wok or saucepan, add the contents of the mortar or food processor, and fry until the nuts begin to brown, for about 1–2 minutes.

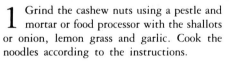

3 Add the shrimp paste or fish sauce and curry paste, followed by the coconut milk, stock cube and curry leaves. Simmer for 10 minutes.

4 Cut the white fish into bite-size pieces. Place the fish and prawns (shrimp) in a large frying basket, immerse into the simmering coconut stock and cook for 3–4 minutes.

Sesame Baked Fish with a Hot Ginger Marinade

Panggang Bungkus

Tropical fish are found increasingly in supermarkets, but oriental foodstores usually have a wider selection.

SERVES 4–6

Ingredients
2 red snapper, parrot fish or monkfish tails,
   weighing about 350g/12oz each
2 tbsp vegetable oil
2 tsp sesame oil
2 tbsp sesame seeds
1 piece fresh ginger, 2.5cm/1in long, peeled and
   thinly sliced
2 cloves garlic, crushed
2 small red chillies, seeded and finely chopped
4 shallots or 1 medium onion, halved and sliced
2 tbsp water
1 piece shrimp paste, 12mm/½in square, or 1 tbsp
   fish sauce
2 tsp sugar
½ tsp cracked black pepper
juice of 2 limes
3–4 banana leaves, or aluminium foil
1 lime, to garnish
2 red chilli flowers, to garnish

1 Clean the fish inside and out under cold running water. Pat dry with kitchen paper. Slash both sides of each fish deeply with a knife to enable the marinade to penetrate effectively. If using parrot fish, rub with fine salt and leave to stand for 15 minutes. (This will remove the chalky coral flavour often associated with the fish.)

2 To make the marinade, heat the vegetable and sesame oils in a wok, add the sesame seeds and fry until golden. Add the ginger, garlic, chillies and shallots or onion and soften over a gentle heat without burning. Add the water, shrimp paste or fish sauce, sugar, pepper and lime juice, simmer for 2–3 minutes and allow to cool.

3 If using banana leaves, remove the central stem and discard. Soften the leaves by dipping in boiling water. To keep them supple, rub all over with vegetable oil. Spread the marinade over the fish, wrap in the banana leaf and fasten with a bamboo skewer, or wrap the fish in foil. Leave the fish in a cool place to allow the flavours to mingle, for up to 3 hours.

4 Preheat the oven to 180°C/350°F/Gas Mark 4 or light a barbecue and allow the embers to settle to a steady glow. Place the wrapped fish on a wire rack or baking sheet and cook for 35–40 minutes.

SPICY CLAY-POT CHICKEN

Ayam Golek

Clay-pot cooking stems from the practice of burying a glazed pot in the embers of an open fire. The gentle heat surrounds the base and keeps the liquid inside at a slow simmer, similar to the modern-day casserole.

SERVES 4–6

Ingredients
1 × 1.5kg/3½lb chicken
3 tbsp freshly-grated coconut
2 tbsp vegetable oil
2 shallots, or 1 small onion, finely chopped
2 cloves garlic, crushed

1 piece lemon grass, 5cm/2in long
1 piece galingal or fresh ginger, 2.5cm/1in long, peeled and thinly sliced
2 small green chillies, seeded and finely chopped
1 piece shrimp paste, 12mm/½in square, or 1 tbsp fish sauce
400g/14fl oz canned coconut milk
300ml/½ pint/1¼ cups chicken stock

2 lime leaves (optional)
1 tbsp sugar
1 tbsp rice or white wine vinegar
2 ripe tomatoes, to garnish
2 tbsp chopped coriander leaves, to garnish
boiled rice, to serve

1 To joint the chicken, remove the legs and wings with a chopping knife. Skin the pieces and divide the drumsticks from the thighs and, using a pair of kitchen scissors, remove the lower part of the chicken leaving the breast piece. Remove as many of the bones as you can, to make the dish easier to eat. Cut the breast piece into 4 and set aside.

2 Dry-fry the coconut in a large wok until evenly brown. Add the vegetable oil, shallots or onion, garlic, lemon grass, galingal or ginger, chillies and shrimp paste or fish sauce. Fry briefly to release the flavours. Preheat the oven to 180°C/350°F/Gas Mark 4. Add the chicken joints to the wok and brown evenly with the spices for 2–3 minutes.

3 Strain the coconut milk, and add the thin part with the chicken stock, lime leaves if using, sugar and vinegar. Transfer to a glazed clay pot, cover and bake for 50–55 minutes or until the chicken is tender. Stir in the thick part of the coconut milk and return to the oven for 5–10 minutes to simmer and thicken.

4 Place the tomatoes in a bowl and cover with boiling water to loosen and remove the skins. Halve the tomatoes, remove the seeds and cut into large dice. Add the tomatoes to the finished dish, scatter with the chopped coriander and serve with a bowl of rice.

GREEN VEGETABLE SALAD WITH COCONUT MINT DIP

Syabas

This dish is served as an accompaniment to Singapore and Malaysian meat dishes.

SERVES 4–6	115g/4oz Chinese leaves, roughly shredded	2 tsp sugar
	115g/4oz bean sprouts	3 tbsp creamed coconut
Ingredients	lettuce leaves, to serve	75ml/5 tbsp/⅓ cup boiling water
115g/4oz mange-tout (snow peas), topped and tailed and halved		2 tsp fish sauce
	Dipping sauce	3 tbsp vegetable oil
114g/4oz French beans, trimmed and halved	1 clove garlic, crushed	juice of 1 lime
½ cucumber, peeled, halved and sliced	1 small green chilli, seeded and finely chopped	2 tbsp freshly-chopped mint

1 Bring a saucepan of salted water to the boil. Blanch the mange-tout (snow peas), beans and cucumber for 4 minutes. Refresh under cold running water. Drain and set aside.

2 To make the dressing, pound the garlic, chilli and sugar together using a pestle and mortar. Add the coconut, water, fish sauce, vegetable oil, lime juice and mint.

3 Pour the dressing into a shallow bowl and serve with the salad ingredients arranged in an open basket.

SIZZLING STEAK

Daging

This method of sizzling meat on a hot grill can also be applied to sliced chicken or pork.

SERVES 4–6	2 tsp whole black peppercorns	**Dipping sauce**
	1 tbsp sugar	75ml/5 tbsp/⅓ cup beef stock
Ingredients	2 tbsp tamarind sauce	2 tbsp tomato sauce (ketchup)
4 × 200g/7oz rump steaks	3 tbsp dark soy sauce	1 tsp chilli sauce
1 clove garlic, crushed	1 tbsp oyster sauce	juice of 1 lime
1 piece fresh ginger, 2.5cm/1in long, peeled and finely chopped	vegetable oil, for brushing	

1 Pound and blend all the ingredients together. Pour the marinade over the beef and allow the flavours to mingle for up to 8 hours.

2 Heat a cast iron grilling plate over a high heat. Scrape the marinade from the meat and reserve. Brush the meat with oil and cook for 2 minutes on each side, or as you prefer.

3 Place the marinade in a pan, add the stock, sauces and lime juice and simmer briefly. Serve the steaks and the dipping sauce separately.

CHICKEN SATE WITH PEANUT SAUCE

Sate Ayam Saos Kacang

Both the marinated chicken and sauce can be stored in the freezer for up to 6 weeks. Allow 2 hours to thaw.

SERVES 4–6

Ingredients
4 chicken breast fillets
1 tbsp coriander seeds
2 tsp fennel seeds
2 cloves garlic, crushed
1 piece lemon grass, 5cm/2in long, shredded
½ tsp turmeric
2 tsp sugar
½ tsp salt
2 tbsp soy sauce

1 tbsp sesame oil
juice of ½ lime
lettuce leaves, to serve
1 bunch mint leaves, to garnish
1 lime, quartered, to garnish
½ cucumber, quartered, to garnish

Sauce
150g/5oz raw peanuts
1 tbsp vegetable oil
2 shallots, or 1 small onion, finely chopped
1 clove garlic, crushed

1–2 small chillies, seeded and finely chopped
1 piece shrimp paste, 12mm/½in square, or 1 tbsp fish sauce
2 tbsp tamarind sauce
100ml/4fl oz/½ cup coconut milk
1 tbsp honey

1 Cut the chicken into long thin strips and thread, zig-zag, onto 12 bamboo skewers. Arrange on a flat plate and set aside.

2 To make the marinade, dry-fry the coriander and fennel seeds in a wok. Grind smoothly using a pestle and mortar or food processor, then add to the wok with the garlic, lemon grass, turmeric, sugar, salt, soy sauce, sesame oil and lime juice. Allow the mixture to cool. Spread it over the chicken and leave in a cool place for up to 8 hours.

3 To make the peanut sauce, fry the peanuts in a wok with a little oil, or place under a moderate grill (broiler), tossing them all the time to prevent burning. Turn the peanuts out onto a clean cloth and rub vigorously with your hands to remove the papery skins. Place the peanuts in a food processor and blend for 2 minutes.

4 Heat the vegetable oil in a wok, and soften the shallots or onion, garlic and chillies. Add the shrimp paste or fish sauce together with the tamarind sauce, coconut milk and honey. Simmer briefly, add to the peanuts and process to form a thick sauce. Heat the grill (broiler) to moderately hot. If using a barbecue, let the embers settle to a white glow. Brush the chicken with a little vegetable oil and grill for 6–8 minutes. Serve on a bed of lettuce, garnished, and with a bowl of dipping sauce.

HOT CHILLI CRAB WITH GINGER AND LIME

Ikan Maris

Serve this dish with a bowl of chopped cucumber and hot slices of toast.

SERVES 4–6

Ingredients
2 medium crabs, cooked
1 piece fresh ginger, 2.5cm/1in long, peeled and chopped
2 cloves garlic, crushed
1–2 small red chillies, seeded and finely chopped
1 tbsp sugar
2 tbsp vegetable oil
4 tbsp tomato sauce (ketchup)

150ml/¼ pint/⅔ cup water
juice of 2 limes
2 tbsp freshly-chopped coriander leaves, to garnish

Cook's tip

Hot towels are useful towards the end of the meal to clean messy fingers. To prepare your own, moisten white flannels with cologne-scented water, wrap in a plastic bag and microwave for 2 minutes at full power. Remove from the bag and bring to the table in a covered basket.

1 To prepare the crab, twist off the legs and claws. Crack open the thickest part of the shell with a hammer or the back of a heavy knife.

2 Prise off the underside leg section with your two thumbs. From this section, remove the stomach sac and the grey gills, and discard. Cut the section into 4 with a knife. Cut the upper shell into 6 equal pieces.

3 Pound the ginger, garlic, chillies and sugar using a pestle and mortar. Heat the vegetable oil in a large wok, add the pounded spices and fry gently for about 1–2 minutes. Add the tomato sauce (ketchup), water and lime juice and simmer briefly.

4 Add the pieces of crab and heat through for 3–4 minutes. Turn out into a serving bowl and scatter with the chopped coriander.

MALAYSIAN FISH CURRY

Ikan Moolee

Hot Tomato Sambal is often served as an accompaniment to this dish.

SERVES 4–6	1 piece galingal or fresh ginger, 2.5cm/1in long, peeled and thinly sliced	575ml/1 pint/2½ cups chicken stock
Ingredients	2 small red chillies, seeded and finely chopped	½ tsp turmeric
700g/1½lb monkfish, hokey or red snapper fillet	2 cloves garlic, crushed	3 tsp sugar
salt, to season	1 piece lemon grass, 5cm/2in long, shredded	juice of 1 lime, or ½ lemon
3 tbsp freshly-grated or desiccated (shredded) coconut	1 piece shrimp paste, 12mm/½in square, or 1 tbsp fish sauce	
2 tbsp vegetable oil	400g/14oz canned coconut milk	

1 Cut the fish into large chunks, season with salt and set aside.

2 Dry-fry the coconut in a large wok until evenly brown. Add the vegetable oil, galingal or ginger, chillies, garlic and lemon grass and fry briefly. Stir in the shrimp paste or fish sauce. Strain the coconut milk in a sieve, then add the thin coconut milk.

3 Add the chicken stock, turmeric, sugar, a little salt and the lime or lemon juice. Simmer for 10 minutes. Add the fish and simmer for 6–8 minutes. Stir in the thick part of the coconut milk, simmer to thicken, and serve with rice.

PLAIN BOILED RICE

A small amount of vegetable oil added to the rice will enhance its natural flavour.

SERVES 4–6
Ingredients
400g/14oz long grain rice
1 tbsp vegetable oil
700ml/1¼ pints/3 cups boiling water
½ tsp salt

1 Wash and drain the rice several times in cold water until the water is no longer starchy. Put the rice in a heavy saucepan, add the vegetable oil, water and salt. Stir once to prevent the rice from sticking to the pan and simmer for 10–12 minutes. After this time, remove from the heat, cover and allow the rice to steam in its own heat for a further 5 minutes. Fluff the rice with a fork or chopsticks before serving.

COCONUT RICE WITH LEMON GRASS

Serve this rice dish with Sizzling Steak or other meat dishes.

SERVES 4–6	½ tsp salt
	1 piece lemon grass, 5cm/2in long
Ingredients	25g/1oz creamed coconut
400g/14oz long grain rice	700ml/1¼ pints/3 cups boiling water

1 Wash and drain the rice several times in cold water until the water is no longer starchy. Put the rice, salt, lemon grass and coconut in a heavy saucepan, cover with the measured amount of boiling water. Stir once to prevent the grains from sticking to the pan, and simmer uncovered for 10–12 minutes.

2 Remove from the heat, cover and allow to steam in its own heat for a further 5 minutes. Fluff the rice with a fork or chopsticks before serving.

SINGAPORE SLING

Singapore Sling is enjoyed in cocktail bars around the world. Recipes vary considerably, but they all use a standard measure that equates to a little less than 2 tbsp.

SERVES I

Ingredients
ice
2 measures gin
I measure cherry brandy

I measure lemon juice
soda water, to taste
I slice orange
I slice lemon
I Maraschino cherry, to garnish
I sprig mint, to garnish

1 Wrap the ice in a clean cloth, and crush with a rolling pin or the underside of a saucepan. Half-fill a cocktail shaker with ice.

2 Add the gin, cherry brandy and lemon juice and shake.

3 Strain the mixture into a goblet or tall glass over ice cubes. Top up with soda water, to taste, and decorate with the slices of orange and lemon, and the cherry and mint.

SPECIAL FRIED NOODLES

Mee Goreng

Mee Goreng is perhaps the most well-known dish of Singapore. It is prepared from a wide range of ingredients.

SERVES 4–6

Ingredients
275g/10oz egg noodles
I chicken breast fillet, skinned
115g/4oz lean pork
2 tbsp vegetable oil
175g/6oz prawn (shrimp) tails,
    fresh or cooked
4 shallots, or I medium onion, chopped
I piece fresh ginger, 2cm/¾in long,
    peeled and thinly sliced
2 cloves garlic, crushed
3 tbsp light soy sauce
I–2 tsp chilli sauce
I tbsp rice or white wine vinegar
I tsp sugar
½ tsp salt
115g/4oz Chinese leaves, shredded
115g/4oz fresh spinach, shredded
3 spring onions (scallions), shredded

1 Bring a large saucepan of salted water to the boil and cook the noodles according to the instructions on the packet. Drain and set aside. Place the chicken breast and pork in the freezer for 30 minutes to firm but not freeze.

2 Slice the meat thinly against the grain. Heat the oil in a large wok and fry the chicken, pork and prawns (shrimp) for 2–3 minutes. Add the shallots or onion, ginger and garlic and fry without letting them colour.

3 Add the soy and chilli sauces, vinegar, sugar and salt. Bring to a simmer, add the Chinese leaves, spinach and spring onions (scallions), cover and cook for 3–4 minutes. Lastly add the noodles, heat through and serve.

GRILLED (BROILED) FISH WITH A CASHEW GINGER MARINADE

Panggang Bungkus

To capture the sweet spicy flavours of this Indonesian favourite, marinated fish are wrapped in green banana leaves or foil and baked. The packets of fish are brought to the table, releasing a sweet spicy aroma.

SERVES 4

Ingredients
- 1.1kg/2½lb pomfret, parrot fish or sea bass, scaled and cleaned
- 150g/5oz raw cashew nuts
- 2 shallots, or 1 small onion, finely chopped
- 1 piece fresh ginger, 12mm/½in long, peeled and finely chopped
- 1 clove garlic, crushed
- 1 small red chilli, seeded and finely chopped
- 2 tbsp vegetable oil
- 1 tbsp shrimp paste
- 2 tsp sugar
- ½ tsp salt
- 2 tbsp tamarind sauce
- 2 tbsp tomato sauce (ketchup)
- juice of 2 limes
- 4 young banana leaves, or aluminium foil

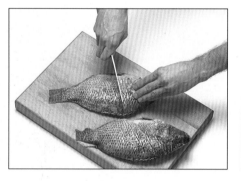

Cook's tip

Banana leaves are readily available from Indian or South-east Asian food stores. However, if these are difficult to obtain, simply wrap each fish in aluminium foil.

For an authentic taste of the Far East, the fish may be barbecued. Light the barbecue and allow the embers to settle to a steady glow. Grill (broil) each fish packet for 30–35 minutes.

1 Slash the fish 3–4 times on each side with a sharp knife to help it cook through to the bone. Set aside.

2 Grind the cashew nuts, shallots or onion, ginger, garlic and chilli to a fine paste using a pestle and mortar or food processor. Add the vegetable oil, shrimp paste, sugar and salt and blend, then add the tamarind sauce, tomato sauce (ketchup) and lime juice.

3 Cover both sides of the fish with the marinade and leave for up to 8 hours to marinate.

4 To soften the banana leaves, remove the thick central stem and immerse the leaves in boiling water for 1 minute. Brush the leaves with vegetable oil. Wrap the fish in a banana leaf fastened with a bamboo skewer, or wrap in foil. Preheat the oven to 180 C/350 F/Gas Mark 4 and bake for 30–35 minutes.

BEEF SATE WITH A HOT MANGO DIP

Sate Bali

Serve this dish with a green salad and a bowl of plain rice.

MAKES 12 SKEWERS

Ingredients
450g/1lb sirloin steak, 2cm/¾ in thick, trimmed
1 tbsp coriander seeds
1 tsp cumin seeds
50g/2oz raw cashew nuts
1 tbsp vegetable oil
2 shallots, or 1 small onion, finely chopped

1 piece fresh ginger, 12mm/½in long, peeled and finely chopped
1 clove garlic, crushed
2 tbsp tamarind sauce
2 tbsp dark soy sauce
2 tsp sugar
1 tsp rice or white wine vinegar

Hot mango dip
1 ripe mango
1–2 small red chillies, seeded and finely chopped
1 tbsp fish sauce
juice of 1 lime
2 tsp sugar
¼ tsp salt
2 tbsp freshly-chopped coriander leaves

1 Slice the beef into long narrow strips and thread, zig-zag, onto 12 bamboo skewers. Lay on a flat plate and set aside.

2 For the marinade, dry-fry the seeds and nuts in a large wok until evenly brown. Place in a pestle and mortar with a rough surface and crush finely. Alternatively, blend the spices and nuts in a food processor. Add the vegetable oil, shallots or onion, ginger, garlic, tamarind and soy sauces, sugar and vinegar. Spread this mixture over the beef and leave to marinate for up to 8 hours. Cook the beef under a moderate grill (broiler) or over a barbecue for 6–8 minutes, turning to ensure an even colour. Meanwhile, make the mango dip.

3 Process the mango flesh with the chillies, fish sauce, lime juice, sugar and salt until smooth, then add the coriander.

PRAWN (SHRIMP) SATE WITH PAW PAW SAUCE

Udang Sate

Fresh prawns (shrimp) are available frozen from reputable fishmongers. Chinese supermarkets also keep a good supply.

MAKES 12 SKEWERS

Ingredients
700g/1½lb whole fresh prawn (shrimp) tails or 24 king prawns (shrimp)
2 tbsp coriander seeds
2 tsp fennel seeds
2 shallots, or 1 small onion, finely chopped
1 piece fresh ginger, 12mm/½in long, peeled and

finely chopped
2 cloves garlic, crushed
1 piece lemon grass, 5cm/2in long
2 tsp creamed coconut
juice of 1 lime
1 tbsp fish sauce
2 tsp chilli sauce
2 tbsp light soy sauce
4 tsp sugar

½ tsp salt
lettuce leaves, to serve

Sauce
2 ripe paw paws or papayas
juice of 1 lime
½ tsp freshly-ground black pepper
pinch of salt
2 tbsp freshly-chopped mint

1 Thread the prawns (shrimp) onto 12 bamboo skewers and lay on a flat plate.

2 Dry-fry the coriander and fennel seeds, then pound smoothly in a pestle and mortar. Add the shallots or onion, ginger, garlic and lemon grass and combine. Lastly add the coconut, lime juice, fish, chilli and soy sauces, sugar and salt. Spread the sauce over the prawns (shrimp) and leave in a cool place for up to 8 hours. Cook the prawns (shrimp) under a moderate grill (broiler) or over a barbecue for 6–8 minutes, turning once.

3 Blend the paw paw, lime juice, pepper and salt. Stir in the mint and serve.

PRAWN (SHRIMP) CURRY WITH QUAILS' EGGS

Gulai Udang

Quails' eggs are available from speciality food shops and delicatessens. Hens' eggs may be substituted if quails' eggs are hard to come by. Use 1 hen's egg to every 4 quails' eggs.

SERVES 4

Ingredients

900g/2lb fresh prawn (shrimp) tails, peeled and de-veined
12 quails' eggs
2 tbsp vegetable oil
4 shallots or 1 medium onion, finely chopped
1 piece galingal or fresh ginger, 2.5cm/1in long, peeled and chopped
2 cloves garlic, crushed
1 piece lemon grass, 5cm/2in long, finely shredded

1–2 small red chillies, seeded and finely chopped
½ tsp turmeric
1 piece shrimp paste, 12mm/½in square, or 1 tbsp fish sauce
400g/14fl oz canned coconut milk
300ml/½ pint/1¼ cups chicken stock
115g/4oz Chinese leaves, roughly shredded
2 tsp sugar
½ tsp salt
2 spring onions (scallions), green part only, shredded, to garnish
2 tbsp shredded coconut, to garnish

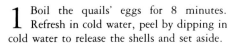

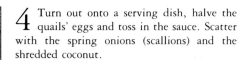

1 Boil the quails' eggs for 8 minutes. Refresh in cold water, peel by dipping in cold water to release the shells and set aside.

2 Heat the vegetable oil in a large wok, add the shallots or onion, galingal or ginger and garlic and soften without colouring. Add the lemon grass, chillies, turmeric and shrimp paste or fish sauce and fry briefly to bring out their flavours.

3 Add the prawns (shrimp) and fry briefly. Pour the coconut milk in a strainer over a bowl, then add the thin part of the milk with the chicken stock. Add the Chinese leaves, sugar and salt and bring to the boil. Simmer for 6–8 minutes.

4 Turn out onto a serving dish, halve the quails' eggs and toss in the sauce. Scatter with the spring onions (scallions) and the shredded coconut.

GRILLED (BROILED) CASHEW NUT CHICKEN

Ayam Bali

This dish comes from the beautiful island of Bali where nuts are widely used as a base for sauces and marinades. Serve with a green salad and a hot chilli dipping sauce such as Hot Chilli and Garlic Dipping Sauce.

SERVES 4–6

Ingredients
4 chicken legs

Marinade
50g/2oz raw cashew or macadamia nuts
2 shallots, or 1 small onion, finely chopped
2 cloves garlic, crushed
2 small red chillies, chopped
1 piece lemon grass, 5cm/2in long
1 tbsp tamarind sauce

2 tbsp dark soy sauce
1 tbsp fish sauce (optional)
2 tsp sugar
½ tsp salt
1 tbsp rice or white wine vinegar
Chinese leaves, to serve
radishes, sliced, to garnish
½ cucumber, sliced, to garnish

1 Using a sharp knife, slash the chicken legs several times through to the bone, chop off the knuckle end and set aside.

2 To make the marinade, place the cashew or macadamia nuts in a food processor or coarse pestle and mortar and grind.

3 Add the shallots or onion, garlic, chillies and lemon grass and blend. Add the remaining marinade ingredients.

4 Spread the marinade over the chicken and leave in a cool place for up to 8 hours. Grill (broil) the chicken under a moderate heat or over a barbecue for 15 minutes on each side. Place on a dish lined with Chinese leaves and garnish with the sliced radishes and cucumber.

INDONESIAN PORK AND PRAWN (SHRIMP) RICE

Nasi Goreng

Nasi Goreng is an attractive way of using up leftovers and appears in many variations throughout Indonesia. Rice is the main ingredient, although almost anything can be added for colour and flavour.

SERVES 4–6

Ingredients
3 eggs
pinch of salt
4 tbsp vegetable oil
6 shallots, or 1 large onion, chopped
2 cloves garlic, crushed
1 piece fresh ginger, 2.5cm/1in long, peeled and chopped
2–3 small red chillies, seeded and finely chopped
1 tbsp tamarind sauce
1 piece shrimp paste, 12mm/½in square, or 1 tbsp fish sauce
½ tsp turmeric
6 tsp creamed coconut
juice of 2 limes
2 tsp sugar
½ tsp salt
350g/12oz lean pork or chicken breast fillets, skinned and sliced
350g/12oz fresh or cooked prawn (shrimp) tails, peeled
175g/6oz bean sprouts
175g/6oz Chinese leaves, shredded
175g/6oz frozen peas, thawed
250g/9oz long grain rice, cooked to make 700g/ 1½lb
1 small bunch coriander or basil, roughly chopped, to garnish

1 In a bowl, beat the eggs with a pinch of salt. Heat a non-stick frying pan over a moderate heat. Pour in the eggs and move the pan around until they begin to set. When set, roll up, slice thinly, cover and set aside.

2 Heat 1 tbsp of the oil in a wok and fry the shallots or onion until evenly brown. Remove from pan, set aside and keep warm.

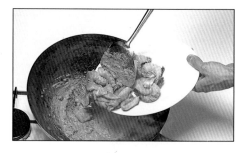

3 Heat the remaining 3 tbsp of oil in the wok, add the garlic, ginger and chillies and soften without colouring. Stir in the tamarind and shrimp paste or fish sauce, turmeric, coconut, lime juice, sugar and salt. Combine briefly over a moderate heat. Add the pork or chicken and prawns (shrimp) and fry for 3–4 minutes.

4 Toss the bean sprouts, Chinese leaves and peas in the spices and cook briefly. Add the rice and stir-fry for 6–8 minutes, stirring to prevent it from burning. Turn out onto a large serving plate, decorate with shredded egg pancake, the fried shallots or onion and chopped coriander or basil.

HOT TOMATO SAMBAL

Sambal Tomat

Sambals are placed on the table as a condiment and are used mainly for dipping meat and fish. They are quite strong and should be used sparingly.

MAKES 120ML/4 FL OZ/½ CUP

Ingredients
3 ripe tomatoes
½ tsp salt
1 tsp chilli sauce
4 tbsp fish sauce, or soy sauce
1 tbsp chopped coriander leaves

1 Cover the tomatoes with boiling water to loosen the skins. Remove the skins, halve, discard the seeds and chop finely.

2 Place the chopped tomatoes in a bowl, add the salt, chilli sauce, fish sauce or soy sauce, and coriander.

HOT CHILLI AND GARLIC DIPPING SAUCE

Sambal Kecap

This sambal is particularly strong, so warn guests who are unaccustomed to spicy foods.

MAKES 120ML/4FL OZ/½ CUP

Ingredients
1 clove garlic, crushed
2 small red chillies, seeded and finely chopped
2 tsp sugar
1 tsp tamarind sauce
4 tbsp soy sauce
juice of ½ lime

1 Pound the garlic, chillies and sugar until smooth using a pestle and mortar, or grind in a food processor.

2 Add the tamarind sauce, soy sauce and lime juice.

CUCUMBER SAMBAL

Sambal Selamat

This sambal has a piquant flavour without the hotness of chillies found in other recipes.

MAKES 150ML/5FL OZ/⅔ CUP

Ingredients
1 clove garlic, crushed
1 tsp fennel seeds
2 tsp sugar
½ tsp salt
2 shallots, or 1 small onion, finely sliced
100ml/4fl oz/½ cup rice or white wine vinegar
¼ cucumber, finely diced

1 Place the garlic, fennel seeds, sugar and salt in a pestle and mortar and pound finely. Alternatively, grind the ingredients thoroughly in a food processor.

2 Stir in the shallots or onion, vinegar and cucumber and allow to stand for at least 6 hours to allow the flavours to combine.

SPICY PEANUT RICE CAKES

Rempeyek

Serve these spicy rice cakes with a crisp green salad and a dipping sauce such as Hot Tomato Sambal.

MAKES 16 PIECES

Ingredients

1 clove garlic, crushed
1 piece fresh ginger, 12mm/½in long, peeled and finely chopped
¼ tsp turmeric
1 tsp sugar
½ tsp salt
1 tsp chilli sauce
2 tsp fish or soy sauce

2 tbsp chopped coriander leaves
juice of ½ lime
115g/4oz long grain rice, cooked
raw peanuts, chopped
150ml/¼ pint vegetable oil, for deep-frying

1 Pound together the garlic, ginger and turmeric using a pestle and mortar. Add the sugar, salt, chilli and fish or soy sauce, coriander and lime juice.

2 Add 85g/3oz of the cooked rice and pound until smooth and sticky. Stir in the remainder of the rice. Wet your hands and shape into thumb-size balls.

3 Roll the balls in chopped peanuts to coat evenly. Set aside until ready to cook and serve.

4 Heat the vegetable oil in a deep frying pan. Prepare a tray lined with kitchen paper to drain the rice cakes. Deep-fry 3 cakes at a time until crisp and golden, remove with a slotted spoon then drain on kitchen paper.

VEGETABLE SALAD WITH A HOT PEANUT SAUCE

Gado Gado

Serve this vegetable salad with Indonesian Pork and Prawn (Shrimp) Rice and Prawn Crackers. The peanut sauce is served separately from the salad, and everyone helps themselves.

SERVES 4–6

Ingredients
2 medium potatoes, peeled
175g/6oz French beans, topped and tailed

Peanut sauce
150g/5oz raw peanuts
1 tbsp vegetable oil
2 shallots, or 1 small onion, finely chopped

1 clove garlic, crushed
1–2 small chillies, seeded and finely chopped
1 piece shrimp paste, 12mm/½in square, or 1 tbsp fish sauce (optional)
2 tbsp tamarind sauce
100ml/4fl oz/½ cup canned coconut milk
1 tbsp clear honey

Salad ingredients
175g/6oz Chinese leaves, shredded

1 iceberg or bib lettuce
175g/6oz bean sprouts
½ cucumber, cut into fingers
150g/5oz giant white radish, shredded
3 spring onions (scallions)
225g/8oz bean curd (tofu), cut into large dice
3 hard-boiled eggs, quartered
1 small bunch coriander

1 Bring the potatoes to the boil in salted water and simmer for 20 minutes. Cook the beans for 3–4 minutes. Drain the potatoes and beans and refresh under cold running water.

2 For the peanut sauce, dry-fry the peanuts in a wok, or place under a moderate grill, tossing them all the time to prevent burning. Turn the peanuts onto a clean cloth and rub vigorously with your hands to remove the papery skins. Place the peanuts in a food processor and blend for 2 minutes.

3 Heat the vegetable oil in a wok, and soften the shallots or onion, garlic and chillies without letting them colour. Add the shrimp paste or fish sauce if using, together with the tamarind sauce, coconut milk and honey. Simmer briefly, add to the peanuts and process to form a thick sauce.

4 Arrange the salad ingredients, potatoes and beans on a large platter and serve with a bowl of the peanut sauce.

TABLE-TOP SIMMER POT

Ta Pin Lo

This meal is well-known in many Eastern countries and serves to unite all members of the family. The idea is to cook or reheat a range of ingredients displayed around a pot of simmering chicken stock. The meal is a great social occasion, and each person chooses their own selection of food. Dipping sauces are provided to season the dishes according to taste.

SERVES 4–6	1.75 litres/3 pints/7½ cups chicken stock
	1 small red chilli, split
Ingredients	1 piece fresh ginger, 2.5cm/1in long, peeled and
175g/6oz lean pork	sliced
175g/6oz fillet steak	175g/6oz Chinese egg noodles, uncooked
1 chicken breast fillet, skinned	225g/8oz Chinese leaves, roughly shredded
225g/8oz white fish fillets (monkfish, halibut or	1 iceberg, bib or cos lettuce, shredded
hokey)	6 spring onions (scallions)
225g/8oz bean curd (tofu)	½ cucumber, sliced
16 fresh prawn (shrimp) tails, peeled and	chilli sauce
de-veined	soy sauce

juice of 3 lemons

1 Place the pork, steak and chicken in the freezer for 30 minutes to firm but not freeze. Slice the meat thinly and arrange on small side dishes.

2 Skin the fish and cut into thick chunks. Cut the bean curd (tofu) into large cubes and place it with the fish and prawns (shrimp) on a small plate.

3 Bring the chicken stock to the boil with the chilli and ginger in a saucepan or casserole that can be served at the table. A flame-lit fondue pot is ideal.

4 Simmer the noodles in a large pan of salted water according to the instructions on the packet. Refresh under cold running water, drain and place in an attractive bowl.

5 Wash all the salad ingredients in water, drain and arrange on separate plates.

6 Place the chilli sauce, soy sauce and lemon juice in three separate small dishes suitable for dipping and serve at the table. Fondue forks are ideal for dipping the meat and noodles, bean curd (tofu) and fish into the stock, although in Singapore little wire baskets are used.

CHICKEN WONTON SOUP WITH PRAWNS (SHRIMP)

Ji Wun Tun Tang

This soup is a more luxurious version of basic Wonton Soup, and is almost a meal in itself.

SERVES 4	2 spring onions (scallions), finely chopped	850ml/1 ½ pints/3¾ cups chicken stock
	1 egg	¼ cucumber, peeled and diced
Ingredients	2 tsp oyster sauce (optional)	1 spring onion (scallion), roughly shredded, to
325g/11oz chicken breast fillet, skin removed	salt and pepper	garnish
200g/7oz prawn (shrimp) tails, fresh or cooked	1 packet wonton skins	4 sprigs coriander leaves, to garnish
1 tsp finely-chopped fresh ginger	1 tbsp cornflour (cornstarch) paste	1 tomato, skinned, seeded and diced, to garnish

1 Place the chicken breast, 150g/5oz prawn (shrimp) tails, ginger and spring onions (scallions) in a food processor and mix for 2–3 minutes. Add the egg, oyster sauce and seasoning and process briefly. Set aside.

2 Place 8 wonton skins at a time on a surface, moisten the edges with flour paste and place ½ tsp of the filling in the centre of each. Fold in half and pinch to seal. Simmer in salted water for 4 minutes.

3 Bring the chicken stock to the boil, add the remaining prawn (shrimp) tails and the cucumber and simmer for 3–4 minutes. Add the wontons and simmer to warm through. Garnish and serve hot.

MALACCA FRIED RICE

Chow Fan

There are many versions of this dish throughout the East, all of which make use of left-over rice. Ingredients vary according to what is available, but prawns (shrimp) are a popular addition.

SERVES 4–6	4 shallots or 1 medium onion, finely chopped	roughly chopped
	1 tsp finely-chopped fresh ginger	225g/8oz frozen peas
Ingredients	1 clove garlic, crushed	225g/8oz thickly sliced roast pork, diced
2 eggs	225g/8oz prawn (shrimp) tails, fresh or cooked	3 tbsp light soy sauce
salt and pepper	1–2 tsp chilli sauce (optional)	350g/12oz long grain rice, cooked
3 tbsp vegetable oil	3 spring onions (scallions), green part only,	

1 In a bowl, beat the eggs well, and season. Heat 1 tbsp of the oil in a large non-stick frying pan, pour in the eggs and allow to set without stirring for less than a minute. Roll up the pancake, cut into thin strips and set aside.

2 Heat the remaining vegetable oil in a large wok, add the shallots, ginger, garlic and prawn (shrimp) tails and cook for 1–2 minutes, ensuring that the garlic doesn't burn.

3 Add the chilli sauce, spring onions (scallions), peas, pork and soy sauce. Stir to heat through, then add the rice. Fry the rice over a moderate heat for 6–8 minutes. Turn into a dish and decorate with the pancake.

PORK AND PEANUT WONTONS WITH PLUM SAUCE

Wanton Goreng

These crispy filled wontons are delicious served with Egg Pancake Salad Wrappers, a popular salad dish of Indonesia. The wontons can be filled and set aside for 8 hours before cooking.

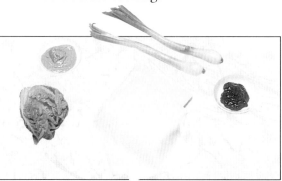

MAKES 40–50 WONTONS

Ingredients

175g/6oz minced (ground) pork, or the
   contents of 175g/6oz fresh pork sausages
2 spring onions (scallions), finely chopped
2 tbsp peanut butter
2 tsp oyster sauce (optional)
salt and pepper

1 packet wonton skins
2 tbsp flour paste
vegetable oil, for deep-frying

Plum sauce
225g/8oz dark plum jam (jelly)
1 tbsp rice or white wine vinegar
1 tbsp dark soy sauce
½ tsp chilli sauce

1 Combine the minced (ground) pork, spring onions (scallions), peanut butter, oyster sauce and seasoning and set aside.

2 For the plum sauce, combine the plum jam (jelly), vinegar, soy and chilli sauces in a serving bowl and set aside.

3 To fill the wonton skins, place 8 wrappers at a time on a work surface, moisten the edges with the flour paste and place ½ tsp of the pork mixture on each one. Fold in half, corner to corner, and twist.

4 Fill a wok or deep frying pan one-third with vegetable oil and heat to 196°C/ 385°F. Have ready a wire strainer or frying basket and a tray lined with kitchen paper. Drop the wontons, 8 at a time, in the hot fat and fry until golden, for about 1–2 minutes. Lift out onto the paper-lined tray and sprinkle with fine salt. Place the plum sauce on a serving plate and surround with the crispy wontons.

HOT CHILLI PRAWNS (SHRIMP)

Udang

Hot Chilli Prawns can be prepared about 8 hours in advance and are best grilled (broiled) or barbecued.

SERVES 4–6

Ingredients
1 clove garlic, crushed
1 piece fresh ginger, 12mm/½in long, peeled and chopped
1 small red chilli, seeded and chopped
2 tsp sugar
1 tbsp light soy sauce
1 tbsp vegetable oil
1 tsp sesame oil
juice of 1 lime
salt, to taste
700g/1½lb whole raw prawns (shrimp)
175g/6oz cherry tomatoes
½ cucumber, cut into chunks
1 small bunch coriander, roughly chopped

---

1 Pound the garlic, ginger, chilli and sugar to a paste using a pestle and mortar. Add the soy sauce, vegetable and sesame oils, lime juice and salt. Cover the prawns (shrimp) with the marinade and allow to marinate for as long as possible, preferably 8 hours.

2 Thread the prawns (shrimp), tomatoes and cucumber onto bamboo skewers. Grill (broil) the prawns (shrimp) for 3–4 minutes, scatter with the coriander and serve.

PRAWN (SHRIMP) CRACKERS

Krupuk

Prawn (Shrimp) Crackers are a popular addition to many Far Eastern dishes and are often served before guests come to the table. Some supermarkets and food stores sell crackers ready for cooking.

SERVES 4–6

Ingredients
300ml/½ pint/1¼ cups vegetable oil
50g/2oz uncooked prawn (shrimp) crackers
fine table salt, to taste

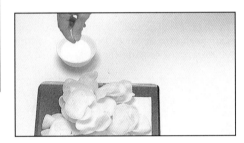

1 Line a tray with kitchen paper. Heat the oil in a large wok until it begins to smoke. Lower the heat to maintain a steady temperature.

2 Drop 3–4 prawn crackers into the oil. Remove from the oil before they begin to colour and transfer to the paper-lined tray. Serve sprinkled with salt.

SWEET AND SOUR GINGER SAMBAL

Sambal Jahe

Sambals are a common sight at Indonesian and Malaysian tables. Their purpose is to perk up or cool down hot chilli flavours. Sambals can also include simple components such as onion and cucumber.

MAKES 90ML/6 TBSP

Ingredients
4–5 small red chillies, seeded and chopped
2 shallots, or 1 small onion, chopped
2 cloves garlic
1 piece fresh ginger, 2cm/¾in long, peeled
2 tbsp sugar
¼ tsp salt
3 tbsp rice or white wine vinegar

1 Finely pound or grind the chillies and shallots or onion together using a pestle and mortar or food processor.

2 Add the garlic, ginger, sugar and salt and continue to grind until smooth. Lastly add the vinegar, combine and pour into a screw-top jar.

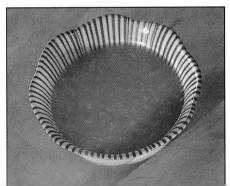

SPICY PORK WITH LEMON GRASS AND COCONUT

Semur Daging

Serve this dish with plain boiled rice and Hot Tomato Sambal.

SERVES 4–6	4 shallots, or 1 medium onion, chopped	300ml/½ pint/1¼ cups chicken stock
	1 piece lemon grass, 5cm/2in long, finely shredded	1 tsp sugar
Ingredients	1–2 small red chillies, seeded and finely chopped	juice of 1 lemon
700g/1½lb lean pork, loin or fillet	1 piece shrimp paste, 12mm/½in square	zest of 1 satsuma, finely shredded
2 tbsp vegetable oil	400g/14oz canned coconut milk	1 small bunch coriander, chopped

3 Add the coconut milk, chicken stock, sugar and lemon juice, return to the boil and simmer for 15–20 minutes. Turn the pork out into a serving dish and sprinkle with the zest of the satsuma and the coriander.

1 Place the pork in the freezer for 30 minutes. Slice the meat thinly.

2 Heat the vegetable oil in a large wok, add the shallots or onion, lemon grass, chillies and shrimp paste. Add the pork and seal.

EGG PANCAKE SALAD WRAPPERS

Nonya Popiah

One of Indonesia's favourite snack foods, pancakes are assembled according to taste and dipped in various sauces.

MAKES 12	1 iceberg or bib lettuce	1 small red chilli, seeded and finely chopped
	115g/4oz bean sprouts	1 tbsp rice or white wine vinegar
Ingredients		2 tsp sugar
2 eggs	**Filling**	115g/4oz giant white radish, peeled and grated
½ tsp salt	3 tbsp vegetable oil	1 medium carrot, grated
1 tsp vegetable oil, plus a little for frying	1 piece fresh ginger, 12mm/½in long, peeled and chopped	115g/4oz Chinese leaf or white cabbage, shredded
115g/4oz plain (all-purpose) flour	1 clove garlic, crushed	2 shallots, or 1 small red onion, thinly sliced
300ml/½ pint/1¼ cups water		

1 Break the eggs into a bowl, add the salt, vegetable oil and flour and stir until smooth. Do not over-mix. Add the water a little at a time and strain into a jug. Allow the batter to stand for 15–20 minutes.

2 Moisten a small non-stick frying pan with vegetable oil and heat. Cover the base of the pan with batter and cook for 30 seconds. Turn over and cook briefly. Stack the pancakes on a plate, cover and keep warm.

3 Heat the oil in a large wok, add the ginger, garlic and chilli and fry gently. Add the vinegar, sugar, white radish, carrot, Chinese leaf and shallots. Cook for 3–4 minutes. Serve with the pancakes and salad.

FILIPINO CHICKEN POT

Puchero

This nourishing main course soup is one of many brought to the Philippines by the Spanish in the sixteenth century. The recipe and method are based on Potajes, a special stew still enjoyed throughout much of Spain. In the Philippines, ingredients vary according to what is available, but the dish still retains much of its original character.

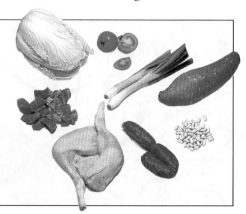

SERVES 4–6

Ingredients
175g/6oz dried haricot beans
3 chicken legs
1 tbsp vegetable oil
350g/12oz lean pork, diced
1 chorizo (optional)
1 small carrot, peeled and roughly chopped
1 medium onion, roughly chopped
1.7 litres/3 pints/7½ cups water
1 clove garlic, crushed

2 tbsp tomato purée (paste)
1 bay leaf
2 chicken stock cubes
350g/12oz sweet potatoes or new potatoes, peeled
2 tsp chilli sauce
2 tbsp white wine vinegar
3 firm tomatoes, skinned, seeded and chopped
225g/8oz Chinese leaves
salt and freshly-ground black pepper
3 spring onions (scallions), shredded
boiled rice, to serve

1 Soak the beans in plenty of cold water for 8 hours. Drain.

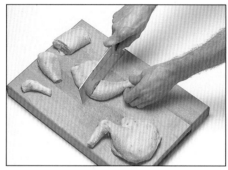

2 Divide the chicken drumsticks from the thighs. Chop off the narrow end of each drumstick and discard.

3 Heat the vegetable oil in a wok or large saucepan, add the chicken, pork, sliced chorizo if using, carrot and onion, then brown evenly.

4 Drain the haricot beans, and add with the water, garlic, tomato purée (paste) and bay leaf. Bring to the boil and simmer for 2 hours until the beans are almost tender.

5 Crumble in the chicken stock cubes, add the sweet or new potatoes and the chilli sauce, then simmer for 15–20 minutes until the potatoes are cooked.

6 Add the vinegar, tomatoes and Chinese leaves, then simmer for 1–2 minutes. Season to taste with salt and pepper. The Puchero is intended to provide enough liquid to be served as a first course broth. This is followed by a main course of the meat and vegetables scattered with the shredded spring onions (scallions). Serve with rice as an accompaniment.

Sweet and Sour Pork with Coconut Sauce

Adobo

Adobo is a popular dish of the Philippines. Typically the meat is tenderized in a marinade before being cooked in coconut milk, shallow-fried and returned to the sauce. Beef, chicken and fish Adobos are also popular.

SERVES 4–6

Ingredients
700g/1 ½lb lean pork, diced
1 clove garlic, crushed
1 tsp paprika
1 tsp cracked black pepper

1 tbsp sugar
175ml/6fl oz/⅔ cup palm or cider vinegar
2 small bay leaves
425ml/15fl oz/1¼ cups chicken stock
50g/2oz creamed coconut
150ml/¼ pint/⅔ cup vegetable oil or lard (shortening), for frying

1 under-ripe papaya or paw paw, peeled, deseeded and roughly chopped
salt
½ cucumber, peeled and cut into sticks
2 firm tomatoes, skinned, seeded and chopped
1 small bunch chives, chopped

1 Marinate the pork, garlic, paprika, black pepper, sugar, vinegar and bay leaves for 2 hours. Add the stock and coconut.

2 Simmer gently for 30–35 minutes, remove pork, and drain. Heat the oil and brown the pork evenly. Remove and drain.

3 Return the pork to the sauce with the papaya or paw paw, season and simmer for 15–20 minutes. Add garnishes and serve.

Noodles with Chicken, Prawns (Shrimp) and Ham

Pansit Guisado

Egg noodles can be cooked up to 24 hours in advance and kept in a bowl of cold water.

SERVES 4–6

Ingredients
285g/10oz dried egg noodles
1 tbsp vegetable oil
1 medium onion, chopped
1 clove garlic, crushed
1 piece fresh ginger, peeled and chopped

50g/2oz canned water chestnuts, sliced
1 tbsp light soy sauce
2 tbsp fish sauce, or strong chicken stock
175g/6oz cooked chicken breast, sliced
150g/5oz cooked ham, thickly sliced, cut into short fingers
225g/8oz prawn (shrimp) tails, cooked and peeled
175g/6oz bean sprouts

200g/7oz canned baby corn-cobs, drained
2 limes, cut into wedges, to garnish
1 small bunch coriander, shredded, to garnish

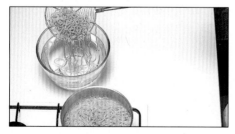

1 Cook the noodles according to the packet. Drain and set aside.

2 Fry the onion, garlic and ginger until soft. Add the chestnuts, sauces and meat.

3 Add the noodles, bean sprouts and corn-cobs. Stir-fry for 6–8 minutes.

BRAISED BEEF IN A RICH PEANUT SAUCE

Kari Kari

Like many dishes brought to the Philippines by the Spanish, this slow-cooking Estofado, renamed Kari Kari, retains much of its original charm. Rice and peanuts are used to thicken the juices, yielding a rich glossy sauce.

SERVES 4–6	2 medium onions, chopped	2 tbsp tamarind sauce
Ingredients	2 cloves garlic, crushed	2 tsp sugar
900g/2lb stewing (braising) chuck, shin or blade steak	285g/10oz celeriac or swede (rutabaga), peeled and roughly chopped	1 bay leaf
2 tbsp vegetable oil	425ml/15fl oz/1¾ cups beef stock	1 sprig thyme
1 tbsp annatto seeds, or 1 tsp paprika and a pinch of turmeric	350g/12oz new potatoes, peeled and cut into large dice	3 tbsp long grain rice, soaked in water
	1 tbsp fish or anchovy sauce	50g/2oz peanuts or 2 tbsp peanut butter
		1 tbsp white wine vinegar
		salt and freshly-ground black pepper, to taste

1 Cut the beef into 2.5cm/1in cubes and set aside. Heat the vegetable oil in a flame-proof casserole, add the annatto seeds if using, and stir to colour the oil dark red. Remove the seeds with a slotted spoon and discard. If you are not using annatto seeds, paprika and turmeric can be added later.

2 Soften the onions, garlic and the celeriac or swede (rutabaga) in the oil without letting them colour. Add the beef and seal to keep in the flavour. If you are not using annatto seeds to redden the sauce, stir the paprika and turmeric in with the beef. Add the beef stock, potatoes, fish or anchovy and tamarind sauces, sugar, bay leaf and thyme. Bring to a simmer and allow to cook on top of the stove for 2 hours.

3 Cover the rice with cold water and leave to stand for 30 minutes. Roast the peanuts under a hot grill (broiler), if using, then rub the skins off in a clean cloth. Drain the rice and grind with the peanuts or peanut butter using a pestle and mortar, or food processor.

4 When the beef is tender, add 4 tbsp of the cooking liquid to the ground rice and nuts. Blend smoothly and stir into the casserole. Simmer gently on the stove to thicken, for about 15–20 minutes. To finish, stir in the wine vinegar and season well with the salt and freshly-ground pepper.

SUGAR BREAD ROLLS

Ensaimadas

In the Philippines, pots of coffee and hot milky chocolate are brought out for a special custom called the merienda. Meriendas occur morning and afternoon and call for a lavish display of cakes and breads. Many are flavoured with sweet coconut although these delicious rolls of Spanish origin are enriched with butter, eggs and cheese.

MAKES 10 ROLLS

Ingredients
350g/12oz strong white bread flour
1 tsp salt
1 tbsp caster (superfine) sugar
150ml/¼ pint/⅔ cup hand-hot water
1 tsp dried yeast
3 egg yolks
50g/2oz unsalted (sweet) butter, softened
85g/3oz Cheddar cheese, grated
6 tsp unsalted (sweet) butter, melted
50g/2oz sugar

1 Sift the flour, salt and caster (superfine) sugar into a food processor fitted with a dough blade or an electric mixer fitted with a dough hook, then make a well in the centre. Dissolve the yeast into the hand-hot water and pour into the well. Add the egg yolks and leave for a few minutes until bubbles appear on the surface of the liquid.

2 Combine the ingredients for less than a minute into a firm dough. Add the 50g/2oz of butter and knead until smooth, for about 2–3 minutes, or 4–5 minutes if using an electric mixer. Turn the dough out into a floured bowl, cover and leave to rise in a warm place until it doubles in volume.

3 Preheat the oven to 190°C/375°F Gas Mark 5. Turn the dough out onto a lightly-floured work surface and divide into 10 pieces. Spread the grated cheese over the surface and roll each of the pieces into 12.5cm/5in lengths. Coil into snail shapes and place on a lightly-greased, high-sided tray or pan measuring 30 × 20cm/12 × 8in.

4 Cover the tray with a loose-fitting plastic bag and leave to rise for a second time until the dough doubles in volume, for about 45 minutes, or up to 2 hours if conditions are not warm. Bake for 20–25 minutes. Brush with the melted butter, sprinkle with the sugar and allow to cool. Break up the rolls and serve in a lined basket.

SWEET AND SOUR PORK AND PRAWN (SHRIMP) SOUP

Sinegang

This main course soup has a sour, rich flavour. Under-ripe fruits and vegetables provide a special tartness.

SERVES 4–6

Ingredients
350g/12oz lean pork, diced
225g/8oz raw or cooked prawn (shrimp) tails, peeled
2 tbsp tamarind sauce
juice of 2 limes

1 small green guava, peeled, halved and seeded
1 small, under-ripe mango, peeled, flesh removed and chopped
1.4 litres/2½ pints/6¼ cups chicken stock
1 tbsp fish or soy sauce
285g/10oz sweet potato, peeled and cut into even pieces
225g/8oz unripe tomatoes, quartered

115g/4oz green beans, topped, tailed and halved
1 star fruit, thickly sliced
85g/3oz green cabbage, shredded
salt
1 tsp crushed black pepper
2 spring onions (scallions), shredded, to garnish
2 limes, quartered, to garnish

1 Trim the pork, peel the prawns (shrimp) and set aside. Measure the tamarind sauce and lime juice into a saucepan.

2 Add the pork, guava and mango. Pour in the stock. Add the fish or soy sauce and simmer, uncovered, for 30 minutes.

3 Add the remaining fruit, vegetables and prawns (shrimp). Simmer for 10–15 minutes. Adjust seasoning, garnish and serve.

SAVOURY PORK PIES

Empanadas

These are native to Galicia in Spain and were brought to the Philippines in the sixteenth century.

MAKES 12 PASTRIES

Ingredients
350g/12oz frozen pastry, thawed

Filling
1 tbsp vegetable oil
1 medium onion, chopped
1 clove garlic, crushed
1 tsp thyme
115g/4oz minced (ground) pork
1 tsp paprika
salt and freshly-ground black pepper
1 hard-boiled egg, chopped
1 medium gherkin (pickle), chopped
2 tbsp freshly-chopped parsley
vegetable oil, for deep-frying

1 To make the filling, heat the vegetable oil in a frying pan or wok and soften the onions, garlic and thyme without browning, for about 3–4 minutes. Add the pork and paprika then brown evenly for 6–8 minutes. Season well, turn out into a bowl and cool. When the mixture is cool, add the hard-boiled egg, gherkin (pickle) and parsley.

2 Turn the pastry out onto a floured work surface and roll out to a 37.5cm/15in square. Cut out 12 circles 12.5cm/5in diameter. Place 1 tbsp of the filling on each circle, moisten the edges with a little water, fold over and seal. Heat the vegetable oil in a deep-fryer fitted with a basket, to 196°C/385°F. Place 3 Empanadas at a time in the basket and deep-fry until golden brown. Frying should take at least 1 minute or the inside filling will not be heated through. Serve warm in a basket covered with a napkin.

Sweet Potato and Pumpkin Shrimp Cakes

Ukoy

These delicious fried cakes should be served warm with a fish sauce or a dark soy sauce.

SERVES 4–6

Ingredients

200g/7oz fresh prawn (shrimp) tails, peeled and roughly chopped
200g/7oz strong white bread flour
½ tsp salt

½ tsp dried yeast
175ml/6fl oz/¾ cup hand-hot water
1 egg, beaten
150g/5oz sweet potato, peeled and grated
225g/8oz pumpkin, peeled, seeded and grated
2 spring onions (scallions), chopped
50g/2oz water chestnuts, sliced and chopped

½ tsp chilli sauce
1 clove garlic, crushed
juice of ½ lime
vegetable oil, for deep-frying

1 Sift the flour and salt into a mixing bowl and make a well in the centre. Dissolve the yeast in the water then pour into the well. Pour in the egg and leave for a few minutes until bubbles appear. Mix to a batter.

2 Place the peeled prawns (shrimp) in a saucepan and cover with water. Bring to the boil and simmer for 10–12 minutes. Drain and refresh in cold water. Roughly chop and set aside. Add the sweet potato and pumpkin.

3 Then add the spring onions (scallions), water chestnuts, chilli sauce, garlic, lime juice and prawns (shrimp). Heat a little oil in a large frying pan. Spoon in the batter in small heaps and fry until golden. Drain and serve

FILIPINO HOT CHOCOLATE

Napalet a Chocolate

This luxurious hot chocolate is served for merienda with Sugar Bread Rolls or Coconut Rice Fritters.

SERVES 2

Ingredients
2 tbsp sugar
100ml/4fl oz/½ cup water
115g/4oz best-quality plain (semi-sweet)
   chocolate
200ml/7fl oz/scant 1 cup evaporated milk

1 Measure the sugar and water into a non-stick saucepan. Simmer to make a basic syrup.

2 Break the chocolate into even pieces, add to the syrup and stir until melted.

3 Add the evaporated milk, return to a simmer and whisk to a froth. Divide between 2 tall mugs and serve.

COCONUT RICE FRITTERS

Puto

These delicious fritters can be served any time, with a mug of steaming coffee or chocolate.

MAKES 28 FRITTERS

Ingredients
150g/5oz long grain rice, cooked
2 tbsp coconut milk powder
3 tbsp sugar
2 egg yolks
juice of ½ lemon
85g/3oz desiccated (shredded) coconut
oil, for deep-frying
icing (confectioners') sugar, for dusting

1 Place 85g/3oz of the cooked rice in a pestle and mortar and pound until smooth and sticky. Alternatively, use a food processor. Turn out into a large bowl, combine with the remainder of the rice, the coconut milk powder, sugar, egg yolks and lemon juice. Spread the desiccated (shredded) coconut onto a tray, divide the mixture into thumb-size pieces with wet hands and roll in the coconut into neat balls.

2 Heat a wok or deep-fat fryer fitted with a wire basket to 180°C/350°F. Fry the coconut rice balls, 3–4 at a time, for 1–2 minutes until the coconut is evenly brown. Turn out onto a plate, and dust with icing (confectioners') sugar. Place a wooden skewer in each fritter and serve with milky coffee or hot chocolate at merienda time.

BEEF AND VEGETABLES IN A TABLE-TOP BROTH

Shabu Shabu

Shabu Shabu is the perfect introduction to Japanese cooking and is well suited to party gatherings. The name refers to the swishing sound made as wafer-thin slices of beef, bean curd (tofu), and vegetables cook in a special broth.

SERVES 4–6

Ingredients
450g/1lb sirloin beef, trimmed
1.7 litres/3 pints/7½ cups water
½ sachet of instant Dashi powder, or ½ vegetable stock cube
150g/5oz carrots
6 spring onions (scallions), trimmed and sliced
150g/5oz Chinese leaves, roughly shredded
225g/8oz giant white radish, peeled and shredded

285g/10oz Udon, or fine wheat noodles, cooked
115g/4oz canned bamboo shoots, sliced
175g/6oz bean curd (tofu), cut into large dice
10 shiitake mushrooms, fresh or dried

Sesame dipping sauce
50g/2oz sesame seeds, or 2 tbsp tahini paste
100ml/4fl oz/½ cup instant Dashi stock, or vegetable stock
4 tbsp dark soy sauce
2 tsp sugar

2 tbsp sake (optional)
2 tsp Wasabi powder (optional)

Ponzu dipping sauce
75ml/3 tbsp/⅓ cup lemon juice
1 tbsp rice or white wine vinegar
75ml/3 tbsp/⅓ cup dark soy sauce
1 tbsp Tamari sauce
1 tbsp Mirin, or 1 tsp sugar
¼ tsp instant Dashi powder, or ¼ vegetable stock cube

1 Place the meat in the freezer for 30 minutes until firm but not frozen. Slice the meat with a large knife or cleaver. Arrange neatly on a plate, cover and set aside. Bring the water to the boil in a Japanese donabe, or any other covered flame-proof casserole that is unglazed on the outside. Stir in the Dashi powder or stock cube, cover and simmer for 8–10 minutes. Serve at the table standing on its own heat source.

2 To prepare the vegetables, bring a saucepan of salted water to the boil. Peel the carrots and with a canelle knife cut a series of grooves along their length. Slice the carrots thinly and blanch for 2–3 minutes. Blanch the spring onions (scallions), Chinese leaves and giant white radish for the same time. Arrange the vegetables with the noodles, bamboo shoots and bean curd (tofu). Slice the mushrooms (soak dried mushrooms in boiling water for 3–4 minutes).

3 To make the sesame dipping sauce, dry-fry the sesame seeds, if using, in a heavy frying pan, taking care not to burn them. Grind the seeds smoothly using a pestle and mortar with a rough surface. Alternatively, you can use tahini paste.

4 Add the remaining ingredients, combine well then pour into a shallow dish. Sesame dipping sauce will keep in the refrigerator for 3–4 days.

5 To make the Ponzu dipping sauce, put the ingredients into a screw-top jar and shake well. Provide your guests with chopsticks and individual bowls, so they can help themselves to what they want. Towards the end of the meal, each guest takes a portion of noodles and ladles the well-flavoured stock over them.

Cook's tip

Dashi is the name given to Japan's most common stock. The flavour derives from a special seaweed known as kelp. This light-tasting stock is available in powder form from oriental food stores. Diluted vegetable stock cube is a good substitute for Dashi.

Tahini paste is a purée of toasted sesame seeds that is used mainly in Greek and Turkish cooking. It is available in large supermarkets and specialist food shops.

MISO BREAKFAST SOUP

Miso-shiru

Miso is a fermented bean paste that adds richness and flavour to many of Japan's favourite soups. This soup provides a nourishing start to the day. Miso paste is widely available in health food stores.

MAKES 1.1 LITRES/2 PINTS/5 CUPS	1.1 litres/2 pints/5 cups Dashi, or light stock
	4 tbsp Miso
Ingredients	115g/4oz bean curd (tofu), cut into large dice
3 shiitake mushrooms, fresh or dried	1 spring onion (scallion), green part only, sliced

1 Slice the mushrooms thinly. If they are dried, soak them first in boiling water for 3–4 minutes. Set aside.

2 Bring the Dashi or light vegetable stock to the boil. Stir in the Miso, add the mushrooms and simmer for 5 minutes.

3 Ladle the broth into 4 soup bowls and place the bean curd (tofu) in each. Add the spring onion (scallion) and serve.

CRAB AND BEAN CURD (TOFU) DUMPLINGS

Kami-dofu Iridashi

These little crab and ginger dumplings are served as a delicious side accompaniment.

MAKES 30	¼ tsp salt	50g/2oz giant white radish, finely grated
	2 tsp light soy sauce	
Ingredients	2 tbsp spring onion (scallion), green part only, finely chopped	**Dipping sauce**
115g/4oz frozen white crab meat, thawed	1 piece fresh ginger, 2cm/¾in long, peeled and grated	100ml/4fl oz/½ cup Dashi, or light vegetable stock
115g/4oz bean curd (tofu), drained		3 tbsp Mirin, or 1 tbsp sugar
1 egg yolk	vegetable oil, for deep-frying	3 tbsp dark soy sauce
2 tbsp rice flour, or wheat flour		

1 Squeeze as much moisture out of the crab meat as you can before using. Press the bean curd (tofu) through a fine strainer with the back of a tablespoon and combine with the crab meat in a bowl.

2 Add the egg yolk, rice flour, salt, spring onion (scallion), ginger and soy sauce to the bean curd (tofu) and crab meat and stir to form a light paste. Set aside. To make the dipping sauce, combine the Dashi or stock with the Mirin or sugar and soy sauce.

3 Line a tray with kitchen paper. Heat the vegetable oil to 196°C/385°F. Shape the mixture to make thumb-size pieces. Fry 6 at a time for 1–2 minutes. Drain on the paper. Serve with the sauce and radish.

BARBECUE-GLAZED CHICKEN SKEWERS

Yakitori

Yakitori is popular throughout Japan and is often served as an appetizer with drinks.

MAKES 12 SKEWERS AND 8 WING PIECES

Ingredients
4 chicken thighs, skinned
4 spring onions (scallions), blanched and cut into
    short lengths
8 chicken wings

Basting sauce
4 tbsp sake
75ml/5 tbsp/⅓ cup dark soy sauce
2 tbsp Tamari sauce
3 tbsp Mirin, or sweet sherry
4 tbsp sugar

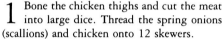

1 Bone the chicken thighs and cut the meat into large dice. Thread the spring onions (scallions) and chicken onto 12 skewers.

2 To prepare the chicken wings, remove the wing tip at the first joint. Chop through the second joint, revealing the two narrow bones. Take hold of the bones with a clean cloth and pull, turning the meat around the bones inside out. Remove the smaller bone and set aside.

3 Measure the basting sauce ingredients into a stainless steel or enamel saucepan and simmer until reduced by two-thirds. Cool. Heat the grill (broiler) to a moderately high temperature. Grill (broil) the skewers without applying any oil. When juices begin to emerge from the chicken baste liberally with the basting sauce. Allow a further 3 minutes for the chicken on skewers and not more than 5 minutes for the wings.

RAW FISH AND RICE PARCELS

Sushi

Sushi is something of an art form in Japan, but with a little practice it is possible to make sushi at home.

MAKES 8–10

Ingredients

Tuna sushi
3 sheets nori (paper-thin seaweed)
150g/5oz freshest tuna fillet, cut into fingers
1 tsp Wasabi, made into a thin paste
    with a little water
6 young carrots, blanched
450g/1lb cooked sushi rice

Salmon sushi
2 eggs
½ tsp salt
2 tsp sugar
5 sheets nori
450g/1lb cooked sushi rice
150g/5oz freshest salmon fillet, cut into fingers
1 tsp Wasabi, made into a thin paste
    with a little water
½ small cucumber, cut into strips

1 To make the tuna sushi, spread half a sheet of nori onto a bamboo mat, lay strips of tuna across the full length and season with the thinned Wasabi. Place a line of blanched carrot next to the tuna and roll tightly. Moisten the edge with water and seal. Place a square of wet greaseproof paper (non-stick baking paper) onto the bamboo mat, then spread evenly with sushi rice. Place the seaweed-wrapped tuna along the centre and wrap tightly, enclosing the seaweed completely. Remove the paper and cut into neat rounds with a wet knife.

2 To make the salmon sushi, make a simple flat omelette by beating together the eggs, salt and sugar. Heat a large non-stick pan, pour in the egg mixture, stir briefly and allow to set. Turn out onto a clean cloth and cool. Place the nori onto a bamboo mat, cover with the omelette and trim to size. Spread a layer of rice over the omelette then lay strips of salmon across the width. Season the salmon with the thinned Wasabi, then place a strip of cucumber next to the salmon. Fold the bamboo mat in half, forming a tear shape inside. Cut into neat sections with a wet knife.

SALT-GRILLED (BROILED) MACKEREL

Shio-yaki

Shio-yaki means salt-grilled. In Japan, salt is applied to oily fish before cooking to draw out the flavours. Mackerel, garfish and snapper are the most popular choices, all of which develop a unique flavour and texture when treated with salt. The salt is washed away before cooking.

SERVES 2	Soy ginger dip	Japanese horseradish
Ingredients	4 tbsp dark soy sauce	3 tsp Wasabi powder
2 small or 1 large mackerel, snapper or garfish, gutted and cleaned, with head on	2 tbsp sugar	2 tsp water
2 tbsp fine sea salt	1 piece fresh ginger, 2.5cm/1 in long, peeled and finely grated	1 medium carrot, peeled and shredded

1 Rinse the fish under cold running water and dry well with kitchen paper. Slash the fish several times on each side, cutting down as far as the bone. This will ensure that the fish will cook evenly. Salt the fish inside and out, rubbing well into the skin. Place the fish on a plate and leave to stand for 40 minutes.

2 To make the soy ginger dip, place the soy sauce, sugar and ginger in a stainless steel saucepan. Simmer for 2–3 minutes, strain and cool. To make the Japanese horseradish, measure the Wasabi powder into a small cup, add the water and stir to make a stiff paste. Shape into a neat ball and place on a heap of shredded carrot.

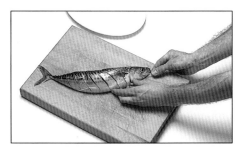

3 Wash the fish in plenty of cold water to remove the salt. Secure each fish in a curved position before grilling. To do this, pass two bamboo skewers through the length of the fish, one above the eye and one below.

4 Preheat a grill (broiler) or barbecue to a moderate temperature and cook the fish for 10–12 minutes, turning once. It is customary to cook the fish plainly, but you may like to baste the skin with a little of the soy ginger dip part way through cooking.

AUBERGINE (EGG PLANT) WITH SESAME CHICKEN

Nasu Hasami-age

Young vegetables are prized in Japan for their sweet, delicate flavour. Here, small aubergines (egg plant) are stuffed with seasoned chicken.

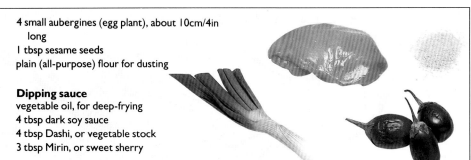

SERVES 4

Ingredients
175g/6oz chicken, breast or thigh, skinned
1 spring onion (scallion), green part only, finely chopped
1 tbsp dark soy sauce
1 tbsp Mirin, or sweet sherry
½ tsp sesame oil
¼ tsp salt

4 small aubergines (egg plant), about 10cm/4in long
1 tbsp sesame seeds
plain (all-purpose) flour for dusting

Dipping sauce
vegetable oil, for deep-frying
4 tbsp dark soy sauce
4 tbsp Dashi, or vegetable stock
3 tbsp Mirin, or sweet sherry

1 To make the stuffing, remove the chicken meat from the bone and mince it finely in a food processor, for about 1–2 minutes. Add the spring onion (scallion), soy sauce, Mirin or sherry, sesame oil and salt.

2 Make 4 slits in the aubergines (egg plant) so they remain joined at the stem. Spoon the minced chicken into the aubergines (egg plant), opening them slightly to accommodate the mixture. Dip the fat end of the stuffed aubergine (egg plant) in the sesame seeds, then dust in flour. Set aside.

3 For the dipping sauce, combine the soy sauce, Dashi or stock and Mirin or sherry. Pour into a shallow bowl and set aside.

4 Heat the vegetable oil in a deep-fryer to 196°C/385°F. Fry the aubergines (egg plant), 2 at a time, for 3–4 minutes. Lift out with a slotted spoon onto kitchen paper.

JAPANESE RICE AND SUSHI RICE

Sushi-meshi

The Japanese prefer their rice slightly sticky so that it can be shaped and eaten with chopsticks. Authentic Japanese rice can be difficult to obtain in the West, but may be replaced by Thai or long grain rice, washed only once to retain a degree of stickiness.

YIELDS 900G/2LB COOKED RICE

Ingredients
350g/12oz Japanese, Thai or long grain rice
1.1 litres/2 pints/5 cups boiling water
1 piece giant kelp, 5cm/2in square (optional)

Dressing
3 tbsp rice vinegar or distilled white vinegar
3 tbsp sugar
2 tsp sea salt

1 If using Japanese rice, wash several times until the water runs clear. Wash Thai or long grain rice only once and drain well. Place the rice in a large heavy saucepan, cover with the measured amount of water and the kelp, if using. Stir once and simmer, uncovered, for 15 minutes. Turn off the heat, cover and stand for a further 5 minutes to allow the rice to finish cooking in its own steam. Before serving, the rice should be fluffed with a rice paddle or spoon. This rice is a Japanese staple.

2 To prepare sushi rice, make the dressing, by heating the vinegar in a small saucepan, with a lid to keep in the strong vapours. Add the sugar and salt and dissolve. Allow to cool. Spread the cooked rice onto a mat or tray and allow to cool.

3 Pour on the dressing and fluff with a rice paddle or spoon. Keep covered until ready to use.

BATTERED FISH, PRAWNS (SHRIMP) AND VEGETABLES

Tempura

Tempura is one of the few dishes brought to Japan from the West. The idea came via Spanish and Portuguese missionaries who settled in southern Japan in the late sixteenth century.

SERVES 4–6

Ingredients
1 sheet nori
8 large raw prawn (shrimp) tails
175g/6oz whiting or monkfish fillet, cut into fingers
1 small aubergine (egg plant)
4 spring onions (scallions), trimmed
6 shiitake mushrooms, fresh or dried
plain (all-purpose) flour, for dusting
vegetable oil, for deep-frying
fine salt, to sprinkle
5 tbsp soy, or Tamari sauce, to serve

Batter
2 egg yolks
300ml/½ pint/1¼ cups iced water
225g/8oz plain (all-purpose) flour
½ tsp salt

De-veining prawns (shrimp)

All raw prawns (shrimp) have an intestinal tract that runs just beneath the outside curve of the tail. The tract is not poisonous but can taste unpleasant. It is therefore best to remove it.

1 Peel the prawn (shrimp) tails leaving the tail part attached.

2 Score each prawn (shrimp) lightly along its length, exposing the tract. Remove the tract with a small knife.

1 Cut the nori into 12mm/½in strips, 5cm/2in long. Moisten one end of the nori with water, and wrap around the tail end of each prawn (shrimp). Skewer the prawns (shrimp) through their length to straighten them. Skewer the fillets of white fish and set aside.

2 Slice the aubergine (egg plant) into neat sections, sprinkle with salt, layer on a plate and press lightly with your hand to expel the bitter juices. Leave for 20–30 minutes, then rinse under cold water. Dry well and place on bamboo skewers. Prepare the other vegetables on skewers and set aside.

3 The batter should be made just before it is used. Beat the egg yolks and half the iced water together in a bowl, sift in the flour and salt and stir loosely with chopsticks without mixing into a dry paste. Add the remainder of the water and stir to make a smooth batter. Avoid over-mixing.

4 Heat the vegetable oil in a deep-fryer or wok, fitted with a wire draining rack, to 180°C/350°F. Dust the fish and vegetables in flour, not more than 3 at a time. Dip into the batter, coating well, then fry in the hot oil until crisp and golden, for about 1–2 minutes. Drain well, sprinkle with fine salt and drain on kitchen paper before serving with a soy or Tamari dipping sauce.

STRAW NOODLE PRAWNS (SHRIMP) IN A SWEET GINGER DIP

Age-mono

Prawns (shrimp) are a popular feature in Japanese cooking. Rarely are they more delicious than when wrapped in crispy noodles and seaweed.

SERVES 4–6	2 sheets nori	**Dipping sauce**
	12 large fresh prawn (shrimp) tails, peeled and de-veined	6 tbsp soy sauce
Ingredients	vegetable oil, for deep-frying	2 tbsp sugar
85g/3oz Somen noodles, or vermicelli		1 piece fresh ginger, 2cm/¾in long, grated

1 Cover the Somen noodles, if using, with boiling water and soak for 1–2 minutes. Drain and dry thoroughly with kitchen paper. Cut the noodles into 7.5cm/3in lengths. If using vermicelli, cover with boiling water for 1–2 minutes to soften. Cut the nori into 12mm/½in strips, 5cm/2in long, and set aside. To make the dipping sauce, bring the soy sauce to the boil with the sugar and ginger. Simmer for 2–3 minutes, strain and cool.

2 Line up the noodles or vermicelli on a wooden board. Straighten each prawn (shrimp) by pushing a bamboo skewer through its length. Roll the prawns (shrimp) in the noodles so that they adhere in neat strands. Moisten one end of the nori and secure the noodles at the fat end of the prawn (shrimp). Set aside.

3 Heat the vegetable oil in a deep-frying pan, or wok fitted with a wire draining rack, to 180°C/350°F. Fry the prawns (shrimp) in the oil, 2 at a time, until the noodles or vermicelli are crisp and golden.

4 To finish, cut through the band of nori with a sharp knife exposing a clean section of prawn (shrimp). Drain on kitchen paper and serve with the dipping sauce in a small dish.

SWEET POTATO AND CHESTNUT CANDIES

Okashi

It is customary in Japan to offer special bean paste candies with tea. The candies tend to be very sweet by themselves, but contrast well with Japanese green teas; in particular, large-leaf Sencha and Banch.

MAKES 18

Ingredients
450g/1lb sweet potato, peeled and roughly chopped
¼ tsp salt

2 egg yolks
200g/7oz sugar
4 tbsp water
75g/5 tbsp rice flour or plain wheat flour
1 tsp orange flower or rose water (optional)
200g/7oz canned chestnuts in heavy syrup, drained

caster (superfine) sugar, for dusting
2 strips candied angelica
2 tsp plum or apricot preserve
3–4 drops red food colouring

1 Place the sweet potatoes in a heavy saucepan, cover with cold water and add the salt. Bring to the boil and simmer until the sweet potatoes are tender, for about 20–25 minutes. Drain well and return to the pan. Mash the sweet potatoes well, or rub through a fine strainer. Place the egg yolks, sugar and water in a small bowl, then combine the flour and orange flower or rose water if using. Add to the purée and stir over a gentle heat to thicken for about 3–4 minutes. Turn the paste out onto a tray and cool.

2 To shape the sweet potato paste, place 2 tsp of the mixture into the centre of a wet cotton napkin or handkerchief. Enclose the paste in the cotton and twist into a nut shape. If the mixture sticks, ensure the fabric is properly wet.

3 To prepare the chestnuts, rinse away the thick syrup and dry well. Roll the chestnuts in caster (superfine) sugar and decorate with strips of angelica. To finish the sweet potato candies, colour the plum or apricot preserve with red colouring and decorate each one with a spot of colour. Serve in a Japanese lacquer box or on an open plate.

Cook's tip

Sugar-coated chestnuts will keep for up to 5 days at room temperature, stored in a sealed box. Sweet potato candies will also keep, sealed and refrigerated.

INDEX

STOCKISTS AND SUPPLIERS

United States

Arizona
Kempo Oriental Market 5595 East 5th Street, Tuscon, Arizona, 85711, (602) 750-9009

Massachusetts
Yoshinoya 36 Prospect Street, Cambridge, Massachusetts, 02139, (617) 491-8221

Minnesota
M.F. Oriental Food 747 Franklin Avenue, Minneapolis, Minnesota, 55404, (612) 870-4002

New York
Katagiri Company 224 East 59th Street, New York, New York, 10022, (212) 755-3566

Siam Grocery 2745 Broadway, New York, New York, 10024, (212) 864 3690

Canada

Dahl's Oriental Food 822 Broadview, Toronto, Ontario, M4K 2P7, (416) 463-8109

Hong Kong Emporium 364 Young Street, Toronto, Ontario, M5B 1S5, (416) 977-3386

U-Can-Buy Oriental Food 5692 Victoria Avenue, Montreal, Quebec, H3W 2P8

New Zealand

Chinese Food Centre Davis Trading Company Ltd, Te Puni Street, Petone, 568-2009

United Kingdom

Duc Cung 122 Upper Clapton Road, London E5,

Golden Gate Hong Kong Ltd 14 Lisle Street, London WC2

Loon Fung Supermarket 42–44 Gerrard Street, London W1

Matahari 102 Westbourne Grove, London W2, (071) 221-7468

Ninjin 244 Great Portland Street, London W1, (071) 388-2511

Sri Thai 56 Shepherds Bush Road, London W6, (071) 602-5760

Australia

Korean, Japanese and Oriental Food Store 14 Oxford Street, Sydney 2000

Oriental Import 406a Brighton Road, Brighton, South Australia

South Africa

Akhalwaya and Sons Gillies Street, Burgersdorp, Johannesburg, (11) 838-1008

Kashmiris Spice Centre 95 Church Street, Mayfair, Johannesburg, (11) 839-3883

Haribak and Sons Ltd 31 Pine Street, Durban (31) 32-662

ACKNOWLEDGEMENTS

The author and publishers would like to thank the following for generously supplying food products and equipment:

B E International Foods Limited
Grafton House
Stockingwater Lane
Enfield
Middlesex EN3

Thanks are also due to the following for their invaluable advice and assistance:

Mrs Duc Cung; Jane Wheeler; Yum Yum Restaurant, London N16